THE
PEACE NEGOTIATIONS
A PERSONAL NARRATIVE

BY

ROBERT LANSING

WITH ILLUSTRATIONS

TOVT
BIEN OV
RIEN

BOSTON AND NEW YORK

HOUGHTON MIFFLIN COMPANY

The Riverside Press Cambridge

1921

CONTENTS

CONTENTS

ILLUSTRATIONS

THE PEACE NEGOTIATIONS

CHRONOLOGY

The Declaration of the Fourteen Points   *January* 18, 1918
Declaration of Four Additional Bases of Peace   *February* 11, 1918
Departure of Colonel House for Paris to represent the
    President on Supreme War Council   *October* 17, 1918
Signature of Armistice, 5 A.M.; effective, 11 A.M.   *November* 11, 1918
Departure of President and American Commission
    for France   *December* 4, 1918
Arrival of President and American Commission in
    Paris   *December* 14, 1918
Meeting of Supreme War Council   *January* 12, 1919
First Plenary Session of Peace Conference   *January* 25, 1919
Plenary Session at which Report on the League of Na-
    tions was Submitted   *February* 14, 1919
Departure of President from Paris for United States   *February* 14, 1919
President lands at Boston   *February* 24, 1919
Departure of President from New York for France   *March* 5, 1919
President arrives in Paris   *March* 14, 1919
Organization of Council of Four   *About March* 24, 1919
President's public statement in regard to Fiume   *April* 23, 1919
Adoption of Commission's Report on League of Na-
    tions by the Conference   *April* 28, 1919
The Shantung Settlement   *April* 30, 1919
Delivery of the Peace Treaty to the German Plenipo-
    tentiaries   *May* 7, 1919
Signing of Treaty of Versailles   *June* 28, 1919
Signing of Treaty of Assistance with France   *June* 28, 1919
Departure of President for the United States   *June* 28, 1919
Departure of Mr. Lansing from Paris for United
    States   *July* 12, 1919
Hearing of Mr. Lansing before Senate Committee on
    Foreign Relations   *August* 6, 1919
Conference of Senate Committee on Foreign Relations
    with the President at the White House   *August* 19, 1919
Hearing of Mr. Bullitt before Senate Committee on
    Foreign Relations   *September* 12, 1919
Return of President to Washington from tour of West   *September* 28, 1919
Resignation of Mr. Lansing as Secretary of State   *February* 13, 1920

THE PEACE NEGOTIATIONS
.·.

CHAPTER I

REASONS FOR WRITING A PERSONAL NARRATIVE

"WHILE we were still in Paris, I felt, and have felt increasingly ever since, that you accepted my guidance and direction on questions with regard to which I had to instruct you only with increasing reluctance. . . .

". . . I must say that it would relieve me of embarrassment, Mr. Secretary, the embarrassment of feeling your reluctance and divergence of judgment, if you would give your present office up and afford me an opportunity to select some one whose mind would more willingly go along with mine."

These words are taken from the letter which President Wilson wrote to me on February 11, 1920. On the following day I tendered my resignation as Secretary of State by a letter, in which I said:

"Ever since January, 1919, I have been conscious of the fact that you no longer were disposed to welcome my advice in matters pertaining to the negotiations in Paris, to our foreign service, or to international affairs in general. Holding these views I would, if I had consulted my personal inclination alone, have resigned as Secretary of State and as a Commissioner to Negotiate Peace. I felt, however, that such a step might have been misinterpreted both at home and abroad, and that it was my duty to cause you no embarrassment in carrying forward the great task in which you were then engaged."

The President was right in his impression that, "while we were still in Paris," I had accepted his guidance and direction with reluctance. It was as correct as my statement that, as early as January, 1919, I was conscious that he was no longer disposed to welcome my advice in matters pertaining to the peace negotiations at Paris.

There have been obvious reasons of propriety for my silence until now as to the divergence of judgment, the differences of opinion and the consequent breach in the relations between President Wilson and myself. They have been the subject of speculation and inference which have left uncertain the true record. The time has come when a frank account of our differences can be given publicity without a charge being made of disloyalty to the Administration in power.

The President, in his letter of February 11, 1920, from which the quotation is made, indicated my unwillingness to follow him in the course which he adopted at Paris, but he does not specifically point out the particular subjects as to which we were not in accord. It is unsatisfactory, if not criticizable, to leave the American people in doubt as to a disagreement between two of their official representatives upon a matter of so grave importance to the country as the negotiation of the Treaty of Versailles. They are entitled to know the truth in order that they may pass judgment upon the merits of the differences which existed. I am not willing that the present uncertainty as to the facts should continue. Possibly some may think that

I have remained silent too long. If I have, it has been only from a sense of obligation to an Administration of which I was so long a member. It has not been through lack of desire to lay the record before the public.

The statements which will be made in the succeeding pages will not be entirely approved by some of my readers. In the circumstances it is far too much to expect to escape criticism. The review of facts and the comments upon them may be characterized in certain quarters as disloyal to a superior and as violative of the seal of silence which is considered generally to apply to the intercourse and communications between the President and his official advisers. Under normal conditions such a characterization would not be unjustified. But the present case is different from the usual one in which a disagreement arises between a President and a high official of his Administration.

Mr. Wilson made our differences at Paris one of the chief grounds for stating that he would be pleased to take advantage of my expressed willingness to resign. The manifest imputation was that I had advised him wrongly and that, after he had decided to adopt a course contrary to my advice, I had continued to oppose his views and had with reluctance obeyed his instructions. Certainly no American official is in honor bound to remain silent under such an imputation which approaches a charge of faithlessness and of a secret, if not open, avoidance of duty. He has, in my judgment, the right to present the case to the American people in order that they may decide whether the imputation was justified by the facts, and whether his conduct was or was not in the circumstances in accord with the best traditions of the public service of the United States.

A review of this sort becomes necessarily a personal narrative, which, because of its intimate nature, is embarrassing to the writer, since he must record his own acts, words, desires, and purposes, his own views as to a course of action, and his own doubts, fears, and speculations as to the future. If there were another method of treatment which would retain the authoritative character of a personal statement, it would be a satisfaction to adopt it. But I know of none. The true story can only be told from the intimate and personal point of view. As I intend to tell the true story I offer no further apology for its personal character.

Before beginning a recital of the relations existing between President Wilson and myself during the Paris Conference, I wish to state, and to emphasize the statement, that I was never for a moment unmindful that the Constitution of the United States confides to the President the absolute right of conducting the foreign relations of the Republic, and that it is the duty of a Commissioner to follow the President's instructions in the negotiation of a treaty. Many Americans, some of whom are national legislators and solicitous about the Constitution, seem to have ignored or to have forgotten this delegation of exclusive authority, with the result that they have condemned the President in intemperate language for exercising this executive right. As to the wisdom of the way in which Mr. Wilson exercised it in directing the negotiations at Paris individual opinions may differ, but as to the legality of his conduct there ought to be but one mind. From first to last he acted entirely within his constitutional powers as President of the United States.

The duties of a diplomatic representative commissioned by the President and given full powers to negotiate a treaty are, in addition to the formal carrying out of his instructions, twofold, namely, to advise the President during the negotiation of his views as to the wise course to be adopted, and to prevent the President, in so far as possible, from taking any step in the proceedings which may impair the rights of his country or may be injurious to its interests. These duties, in my opinion, are equally imperative whether the President directs the negotiations through written instructions issuing from the White House or conducts them in person. For an American plenipotentiary to remain silent, and by his silence to give the impression that he approves a course of action which he in fact believes to be wrong in principle or contrary to good policy, constitutes a failure to perform his full duty to the President and to the country. It is his duty to speak and to speak frankly and plainly.

With this conception of the obligations of a Commissioner to Negotiate Peace, obligations which were the more compelling in my case because of my official position as Secretary of State, I felt it incumbent upon me to offer advice to the President whenever it seemed necessary to me to consider the adoption of a line of action in regard to the negotiations, and particularly so when the indications were that the President purposed to reach a decision which seemed to me unwise or impolitic. Though from the first I felt that my suggestions were received with coldness and my criticisms with disfavor, because they did not conform to the President's wishes and intentions, I persevered in my efforts to induce him to abandon in some cases or to modify in others a course which would in my judgment be a violation of principle or a mistake in policy. It seemed to me that duty demanded this, and that, whatever the consequences might be, I ought not to give tacit assent to that which I believed wrong or even injudicious.

The principal subjects, concerning which President Wilson and I were in marked disagreement, were the following: His presence in Paris during the peace negotiations and especially his presence there as a delegate to the Peace Conference; the fundamental principles of the constitution and functions of a League of Nations as proposed or advocated by him; the form of the organic act, known as the "Covenant," its elaborate character and its inclusion in the treaty restoring a state of peace; the treaty of defensive alliance with France; the necessity for a definite programme which the American Commissioners could follow in carrying on the negotiations; the employment of private interviews and confidential agreements in reaching settlements, a practice which gave color to the charge of "secret diplomacy"; and, lastly, the admission of the Japanese claims to possession of German treaty rights at Kiao-Chau and in the Province of Shantung.

Of these seven subjects of difference the most important were those relating to the League of Nations and the Covenant, though our opposite views as to Shantung were more generally known and more frequently the subject of public comment. While chief consideration will be given to the differences regarding the League and the Covenant, the record would be incomplete if the other subjects were omitted. In fact nearly all of these matters of difference are more or less interwoven and have a collateral, if not a direct, bearing upon one another. They all contributed in affecting the attitude of President Wilson toward the advice that I felt it my duty to volunteer, an attitude which was increasingly impatient of unsolicited criticism and suggestion and which resulted at last in the correspondence of February, 1920, that ended with the acceptance of my resignation as Secretary of State.

The review of these subjects will be, so far as it is possible, treated in chronological order, because, as the matters of difference increased in number, they gave emphasis to the divergence of judgment which existed between the President and myself. The effect was cumulative, and tended not only to widen the breach, but to make less and less possible a restoration of our former relations. It was my personal desire to support the President's views concerning the negotiations at Paris, but, when in order to do so it became necessary to deny a settled conviction and to suppress a conception of the true principle or the wise policy to be followed, I could not do it and feel that to give support under such conditions accorded with true loyalty to the President of the United States.

It was in this spirit that my advice was given and my suggestions were made, though in doing so I believed it justifiable to conform as far as it was possible to the expressed views of Mr. Wilson, or to what seemed to be his views, concerning less important matters and to concentrate on those which seemed vital. I went in fact as far as I could in adopting his views in the hope that my advice would be less unpalatable and would, as a consequence, receive more sympathetic consideration. Believing that I understood the President's temperament, success in an attempt to change his views seemed to lie in moderation and in partial approval of his purpose rather than in bluntly arguing that it was wholly wrong and should be abandoned. This method of approach, which seemed the expedient one at the time, weakened, in some instances at least, the criticisms and objections which I made. It is very possible that even in this diluted form my views were credited with wrong motives by the President so that he suspected my purpose. It is to be hoped that this was the true explanation of Mr. Wilson's attitude of mind, for the alternative forces a conclusion as to the cause for his resentful reception of honest differences of opinion, which no one, who admires his many sterling qualities and great attainments, will willingly accept.

Whatever the cause of the President's attitude toward the opinions which I expressed on the subjects concerning which our views were at variance — and I prefer to assume that the cause was a misapprehension of my reasons for giving them — the result was that he was disposed to give them little weight. The impression made was that he was irritated by opposition to his views, however moderately urged, and that he did not like to have his judgment questioned even in a friendly way. It is, of course, possible that this is not a true estimate of the President's feelings. It may do him an injustice. But his manner of meeting criticism and his disposition to ignore opposition can hardly be interpreted in any other way.

There is the alternative possibility that Mr. Wilson was convinced that, after he had given a subject mature consideration and reached a decision, his judgment was right or at least better than that of any adviser. A conviction of this nature, if it existed, would naturally have caused him to feel impatient with any one who attempted to controvert his decisions and would tend to make him believe that improper motives induced the opposition or criticism. This alternative, which is based of necessity on a presumption as to the temperament of Mr. Wilson that an unprejudiced and cautious student of personality would hesitate to adopt, I mention only because there were many who believed it to be the correct explanation of his attitude. In view of my intimate relations with the President prior to the Paris Conference I feel that in justice to him I should say that he did not, except on rare occasions, resent criticism of a proposed course of action, and, while he seemed in a measure changed after departing from the United States in December, 1918, I do not think that the change was sufficient to justify the presumption of self-assurance which it would be necessary to adopt if the alternative possibility is considered to furnish the better explanation.

It is, however, natural, considering what occurred at Paris, to search out the reason or reasons for the President's evident unwillingness to listen to advice when he did not solicit it, and for his failure to take all the American Commissioners into his confidence. But to attempt to dissect the mentality and to analyze the intellectual processes of Woodrow Wilson is not my purpose. It would only invite discussion and controversy as to the truth of the premises and the accuracy of the deductions reached. The facts will be presented and to an extent the impressions made upon me at the time will be reviewed, but impressions of that character which are not the result of comparison with subsequent events and of mature deliberation are not always justified. They may later prove to be partially or wholly wrong. They have the value, nevertheless, of explaining in many cases why I did or did not do certain things, and of disclosing the state of mind that in a measure determined my conduct which without this recital of contemporaneous impressions might mystify one familiar with what afterwards took place. The notes, letters, and memoranda which are quoted in the succeeding pages, as well as the opinions and beliefs held at the time (of which, in accordance with a practice of years, I kept a record supplementing my daily journal of events), should be weighed and measured by the situation which existed when they were written and not alone in the light of the complete review of the proceedings. In forming an opinion as to my differences with the President it should be the reader's endeavor to place himself in my position at the time and not judge them solely by the results of the negotiations at Paris. It comes to this: Was I justified then? Am I justified now? If those questions are answered impartially and without prejudice, there is nothing further that I would ask of the reader.

CHAPTER II

MR. WILSON'S PRESENCE AT THE PEACE CONFERENCE

EARLY in October, 1918, it required no prophetic vision to perceive that the World War would come to an end in the near future. Austria-Hungary, acting with the full approval of the German Government, had made overtures for peace, and Bulgaria, recognizing the futility of further struggle, had signed an armistice which amounted to an unconditional surrender. These events were soon followed by the collapse of Turkish resistance and by the German proposals which resulted in the armistice which went into effect on November 11, 1918.

In view of the importance of the conditions of the armistice with Germany and their relation to the terms of peace to be later negotiated, the President considered it essential to have an American member added to the Supreme War Council, which then consisted of M. Clemenceau, Mr. Lloyd George, and Signor Orlando, the premiers of the three Allied Powers. He selected Colonel Edward M. House for this important post and named him a Special Commissioner to represent him personally. Colonel House with a corps of secretaries and assistants sailed from New York on October 17, *en route* for Paris where the Supreme War Council was in session.

Three days before his departure the Colonel was in Washington and we had two long conferences with the President regarding the correspondence with Germany and with the Allies relating to a cessation of hostilities, during which we discussed the position which the United States should take as to the terms of the armistice and the bases of peace which should be incorporated in the document.

It was after one of these conferences that Colonel House informed me that the President had decided to name him (the Colonel) and me as two of the American plenipotentiaries to the Peace Conference, and that the President was considering attending the Conference and in person directing the negotiations. This latter intention of Mr. Wilson surprised and disturbed me, and I expressed the hope that the President's mind was not made up, as I believed that if he gave more consideration to the project he would abandon it, since it was manifest that his influence over the negotiations would be much greater if he remained in Washington and issued instructions to his representatives in the Conference. Colonel House did not say that he agreed with my judgment in this matter, though he did not openly disagree with it. However, I drew the conclusion, though without actual knowledge, that he approved of the President's purpose, and, possibly, had encouraged him to become an actual participant in the preliminary conferences.

The President's idea of attending the Peace Conference

was not a new one. Though I cannot recollect the source of my information, I know that in December, 1916, when it will be remembered Mr. Wilson was endeavoring to induce the belligerents to state their objects in the war and to enter into a conference looking toward peace, he had an idea that he might, as a friend of both parties, preside over such a conference and exert his personal influence to bring the belligerents into agreement. A service of this sort undoubtedly appealed to the President's humanitarian instinct and to his earnest desire to end the devastating war, while the novelty of the position in which he would be placed would not have been displeasing to one who in his public career seemed to find satisfaction in departing from the established paths marked out by custom and usage.

When, however, the attempt at mediation failed and when six weeks later, on February 1, 1917, the German Government renewed indiscriminate submarine warfare resulting in the severance of diplomatic relations between the United States and Germany, President Wilson continued to cherish the hope that he might yet assume the rôle of mediator. He even went so far as to prepare a draft of the bases of peace, which he purposed to submit to the belligerents if they could be induced to meet in conference. I cannot conceive how he could have expected to bring this about in view of the elation of the Allies at the dismissal of Count von Bernstorff and the seeming certainty that the United States would declare war against Germany if the latter persisted in her ruthless sinking of American merchant vessels. But I know, in spite of the logic of the situation, that he expected or at least hoped to succeed in his mediatory programme and made ready to play his part in the negotiation of a peace.

From the time that Congress declared that a state of war existed between the United States and the Imperial German Government up to the autumn of 1918, when the Central Alliance made overtures to end the war, the President made no attempt so far as I am aware to enter upon peace negotiations with the enemy nations. In fact he showed a disposition to reject all peace proposals. He appears to have reached the conclusion that the defeat of Germany and her allies was essential before permanent peace could be restored. At all events, he took no steps to bring the belligerents together until a military decision had been practically reached. He did, however, on January 8, 1918, lay down his famous "Fourteen Points," which he supplemented with certain declarations in "subsequent addresses," thus proclaiming his ideas as to the proper bases of peace when the time should come to negotiate.

Meanwhile, in anticipation of the final triumph of the armies of the Allied and Associated Powers, the President, in the spring of 1917, directed the organization, under the Department of State, of a body of experts to collect data and prepare monographs, charts, and maps, covering all historical, territorial, economic, and legal subjects which would probably arise in the negotiation of a treaty of peace. This Commission of Inquiry, as it was called, had its

offices in New York and was under Colonel House so far
as the selection of its members was concerned. The nominal head of the Commission was Dr. Mezes, President of
the College of the City of New York and a brother-in-law
of Colonel House, though the actual and efficient executive
head was Dr. Isaiah Bowman, Director of the American Geographical Society. The plans of organization, the
outline of work, and the proposed expenditures for the
maintenance of the Commission were submitted to me as
Secretary of State. I examined them and, after several
comferences with Dr. Mezes, approved them and recom-
mended to the President that he allot the funds necessary
to carry out the programme.

In addition to the subjects which were dealt with by
this excellent corps of students and experts, whose work
was of the highest order, the creation of some sort of an
international association to prevent wars in the future received special attention from the President as it did from
Americans of prominence not connected with the Government. It caused considerable discussion in the press and
many schemes were proposed and pamphlets written on
the subject. To organize such an association became a
generally recognized object to be attained in the negotiation of the peace which would end the World War; and
there can be no doubt that the President believed more
and more in the vital necessity of forming an effective
organization of the nations to preserve peace in the future
and make another great war impossible.

The idea of being present and taking an active part in formulating the terms of peace had, in my opinion, never been abandoned by President Wilson, although it had remained dormant while the result of the conflict was uncertain. When, however, in early October, 1918, there could no longer be any doubt that the end of the war was approaching, the President appears to have revived the idea and to have decided, if possible, to carry out the purpose which he had so long cherished. He seemed to have failed to appreciate, or, if he did appreciate, to have ignored the fact that the conditions were wholly different in October, 1918, from what they were in December, 1916.

In December, 1916, the United States was a neutral nation, and the President, in a spirit of mutual friendliness, which was real and not assumed, was seeking to bring the warring powers together in conference looking toward the negotiation of "a peace without victory." In the event that he was able to persuade them to meet, his presence at the conference as a pacificator and probably as the presiding officer would not improbably have been in the interests of peace, because, as the executive head of the greatest of the neutral nations of the world and as the impartial friend of both parties, his personal influence would presumably have been very great in preventing a rupture in the negotiations and in inducing the parties to act in a spirit of conciliation and compromise.

In October, 1918, however, the United States was a belligerent. Its national interests were involved; its armies were in conflict with the Germans on the soil of France; its naval vessels were patrolling the Atlantic; and the American people, bitterly hostile, were demanding vengeance on the Governments and peoples of the Central Powers, particularly those of Germany. President Wilson, it is true, had endeavored with a measure of success to maintain the position of an unbiased arbiter in the discussions leading up to the armistice of November 11, and Germany undoubtedly looked to him as the one hope of checking the spirit of revenge which animated the Allied Powers in view of all that they had suffered at the hands of the Germans. It is probable too that the Allies recognized that Mr. Wilson was entitled to be satisfied as to the terms of peace since American man power and American resources had turned the scale against Germany and made victory a certainty. The President, in fact, dominated the situation. If he remained in Washington and carried on the negotiations through his Commissioners, he would in all probability retain his superior place and be able to dictate such terms of peace as he considered just. But, if he did as he purposed doing and attended the Peace Conference, he would lose the unique position which he held and would have to submit to the combined will of his foreign colleagues becoming a prey to intrigue and to the impulses arising from their hatred for the vanquished nations.

A practical view of the situation so clearly pointed to the unwisdom of the President's personal participation in the peace negotiations that a very probable explanation for his determination to be present at the Conference is the assumption that the idea had become so firmly embedded in his mind that nothing could dislodge it or divert him from his purpose. How far the spectacular feature of a President crossing the ocean to control in person the making of peace appealed to him I do not know. It may have been the deciding factor. It may have had no effect at all. How far the belief that a just peace could only be secured by the exercise of his personal influence over the delegates I cannot say. How far he doubted the ability of the men whom he proposed to name as plenipotentiaries is wholly speculative. Whatever plausible reason may be given, the true reason will probably never be known.

Not appreciating, at the time that Colonel House informed me of the President's plan to be present at the Conference, that the matter had gone as far as it had, and feeling very strongly that it would be a grave mistake for the President to take part in person in the negotiations, I felt it to be my duty, as his official adviser in foreign affairs and as one desirous to have him adopt a wise course, to state plainly to him my views. It was with hesitation that I did this because the consequence of the non-attendance of the President would be to make me the head of the American Peace Commission at Paris. There was the danger that my motive in opposing the President's attending the Conference would be misconstrued and that I might be suspected of acting from self-interest rather than from a sense of loyalty to my chief. When, however, the armistice went into effect and the time arrived for completing the personnel of the American Commission, I determined that I ought not to remain silent.

The day after the cessation of hostilities, that is, on November 12, I made the following note:

"I had a conference this noon with the President at the White House in relation to the Peace Conference. I told him frankly that I thought the plan for him to attend was unwise and would be a mistake. I said that I felt embarrassed in speaking to him about it because it would leave me at the head of the delegation, and I hoped that he understood that I spoke only out of a sense of duty. I pointed out that he held at present a dominant position in the world, which I was afraid he would lose if he went into conference with the foreign statesmen; that he could practically dictate the terms of peace if he held aloof; that he would be criticized severely in this country for leaving at a time when Congress particularly needed his guidance; and that he would be greatly embarrassed in directing domestic affairs from overseas."

I also recorded as significant that the President listened to my remarks without comment and turned the conversation into other channels.

For a week after this interview I heard nothing from the President on the subject, though the fact that no steps were taken to prepare written instructions for the American Commissioners convinced me that he intended to follow his original intention. My fears were confirmed. On the evening of Monday, November 18, the President came to my residence and told me that he had finally decided to go to the Peace Conference and that he had given out to the press an announcement to that effect. In view of the publicity given to his decision it would have been futile to have attempted to dissuade him from his purpose. He knew my opinion and that it was contrary to his.

After the President departed I made a note of the interview, in which among other things I wrote:

"I am convinced that he is making one of the greatest mistakes of his career and will imperil his reputation. I may be in error and hope that I am, but I prophesy trouble in Paris and worse than trouble here. I believe the President's place is here in America."

Whether the decision of Mr. Wilson was wise and whether my prophecy was unfulfilled, I leave to the judgment of others. His visit to Europe and its consequences are facts of history. It should be understood that the incident is not referred to here to justify my views or to prove that the President was wrong in what he did. The reference is made solely because it shows that at the very outset there was a decided divergence of judgment between us in regard to the peace negotiations.

While this difference of opinion apparently in no way affected our cordial relations, I cannot but feel, in reviewing this period of our intercourse, that my open opposition to his attending the Conference was considered by the President to be an unwarranted meddling with his personal affairs and was none of my business. It was, I believe, the beginning of his loss of confidence in my judgment and advice, which became increasingly marked during the Paris negotiations. At the time, however, I did not realize that my honest opinion affected the President in the way which I now believe that it did. It had always been my practice as Secretary of State to speak to him with candor and to disagree with him whenever I thought he was reaching a wrong decision in regard to any matter pertaining to foreign affairs. There was a general belief that Mr. Wilson was not open-minded and that he was quick to resent any opposition however well founded. I had not found him so during the years we had been associated. Except in a few instances he listened with consideration to arguments and apparently endeavored to value them correctly. If, however, the matter related even remotely to his personal conduct he seemed unwilling to debate the question. My conclusion is that he considered his going to the Peace Conference was his affair solely and that he viewed my objections as a direct criticism of him personally for thinking of going. He may, too, have felt that my opposition arose from a selfish desire to become the head of the American Commission. From that time forward any suggestion or advice volunteered by me was seemingly viewed with suspicion. It was, however, long after this incident that I began to feel that the President was imputing to me improper motives and crediting me with disloyalty to him personally, an attitude which was as unwarranted as it was unjust.

The President having determined to go to Paris, it

seemed almost useless to urge him not to become a delegate in view of the fact that he had named but four Commissioners, although it had been arranged that the Great
Powers should each have five delegates in the Conference.
This clearly indicated that the President was at least considering sitting as the fifth member of the American group.
At the same time it seemed that, if he did not take his
place in the Conference as a delegate, he might retain in a
measure his superior place of influence even though he was
in Paris. Four days after the Commission landed at Brest
I had a long conference with Colonel House on matters
pertaining to the approaching negotiations, during which
he informed me that there was a determined effort being
made by the European statesmen to induce the President
to sit at the peace table and that he was afraid that the
President was disposed to accede to their wishes. This
information indicated that, while the President had come
to Paris prepared to act as a delegate, he had, after discussing the subject with the Colonel and possibly with
others, become doubtful as to the wisdom of doing so, but
that through the pressure of his foreign colleagues he was
turning again to the favorable view of personal participation which he had held before he left the United States.

In my conversation with Colonel House I told him my
reasons for opposing the President's taking an active part
in the Conference and explained to him the embarrassment that I felt in advising the President to adopt a course
which would make me the head of the American Commis-

sion. I am sure that the Colonel fully agreed with me that it was impolitic for Mr. Wilson to become a delegate, but whether he actively opposed the plan I do not know, although I believe that he did. It was some days before the President announced that he would become the head of the American Commission. I believe that he did this with grave doubts in his own mind as to the wisdom of his decision, and I do not think that any new arguments were advanced during those days which materially affected his judgment.

This delay in reaching a final determination as to a course of action was characteristic of Mr. Wilson. There is in his mentality a strange mixture of positiveness and indecision which is almost paradoxical. It is a peculiarity which it is hard to analyze and which has often been an embarrassment in the conduct of public affairs. Suddenness rather than promptness has always marked his decisions. Procrastination in announcing a policy or a programme makes coöperation difficult and not infrequently defeats the desired purpose. To put off a decision to the last moment is a trait of Mr. Wilson's character which has caused much anxiety to those who, dealing with matters of vital importance, realized that delay was perilous if not disastrous.

Of the consequences of the President's acting as one of his own representatives to negotiate peace it is not my purpose to speak. The events of the six months succeeding his decision to exercise in person his constitutional right to conduct the foreign relations of the United States are in a general way matters of common knowledge and furnish sufficient data for the formulation of individual opinions without the aid of argument or discussion. The important fact in connection with the general topic being considered is the difference of opinion between the President and myself as to the wisdom of his assuming the rôle of a delegate. While I did not discuss the matter with him except at the first when I opposed his attending the Peace Conference, I have little doubt that Colonel House, if he urged the President to decline to sit as a delegate, which I think may be presumed, or if he discussed it at all, mentioned to him my opinion that such a step would be unwise. In any event Mr. Wilson knew my views and that they were at variance with the decision which he reached.

CHAPTER III

GENERAL PLAN FOR A LEAGUE OF NATIONS

IT appears, from a general review of the situation prior and subsequent to the assembling of the delegates to the Peace Conference, that President Wilson's decision to go to Paris and to engage in person in the negotiations was strongly influenced by his belief that it was the only sure way of providing in the treaty of peace for the organization of a League of Nations. While his presence in Paris was probably affected to an extent by other considerations, as I have pointed out, it is to be presumed that he was anxious to participate directly in the drafting of the plan of organization of the League and to exert his personal influence on the delegates in favor of its acceptance by publicly addressing the Conference. This he could hardly have done without becoming a delegate. It would seem, therefore, that the purpose of creating a League of Nations and obtaining the incorporation of a plan of organization in the treaty to be negotiated had much to do with the President's presence at the peace table.

From the time that the United States entered the war in April, 1917, Mr. Wilson held firmly to the idea that the salvation of the world from imperialism would not be lasting unless provision was made in the peace treaty for an international agency strong enough to prevent a future

Woodrow Wilson,

President of the United States of America.

To all who shall see these presents, Greeting:

Know Ye, that reposing special trust and confidence in the Integrity and Ability of Robert Lansing, of New York, I do appoint him a Commissioner Plenipotentiary of the United States of America to Negotiate Peace, and do authorize and empower him to execute and fulfil the duties of that Office according to law and to have and to hold the said Office with all the powers, privileges and emoluments thereunto of right appertaining unto him the said Robert Lansing, during the pleasure of the President of the United States.

In testimony whereof, I have caused these Letters to be made Patent and the Seal of the United States to be hereunto affixed.

Given under my hand at the City of Washington, the thirtieth ——— day of November, in the year of our Lord one thousand nine hundred and eighteen, ——— and of the Independence of the United States of America the one hundred and forty-third. ———

Woodrow Wilson

By the President

Robert Lansing
Secretary of State.

attack upon the rights and liberties of the nations which were at so great a cost holding in check the German armies and preventing them from carrying out their evil designs of conquest. The object sought by the United States in the war would not, in the views of many, be achieved unless the world was organized to resist future aggression. The essential thing, as the President saw it, in order to "make the world safe for democracy" was to give permanency to the peace which would be negotiated at the conclusion of the war. A union of the nations for the purpose of preventing wars of aggression and conquest seemed to him the most practical, if not the only, way of accomplishing this supreme object, and he urged it with earnestness and eloquence in his public addresses relating to the bases of peace.

There was much to be said in favor of the President's point of view. Unquestionably the American people as a whole supported him in the belief that there ought to be some international agreement, association, or concord which would lessen the possibility of future wars. An international organization to remove in a measure the immediate causes of war, to provide means for the peaceable settlement of disputes between nations, and to draw the governments into closer friendship appealed to the general desire of the peoples of America and Europe. The four years and more of horror and agony through which mankind had passed must be made impossible of repetition, and there seemed no other way than to form an international union devoted to the maintenance of peace by composing, as far as possible, controversies which might ripen into war.

For many years prior to 1914 an organization devoted to the prevention of international wars had been discussed by those who gave thought to warfare of the nations and who realized in a measure the precarious state of international peace. The Hague Conventions of 1899 and of 1907 had been negotiated with that object, and it was only because of the improper aspirations and hidden designs of certain powers, which were represented at those great historic conferences, that the measures adopted were not more expressive of the common desire of mankind and more effective in securing the object sought. The Carnegie Endowment for International Peace, the Ginn, now the World, Peace Foundation, and the American Peace Society, and later the Society for the Judicial Settlement of International Disputes, the League to Enforce Peace, and many other organizations in America and in Europe were actively engaged in considering ways and means to prevent war, to strengthen the bonds of international good-will, and to insure the more general application of the principles of justice to disputes between nations.

The outbreak of the war and the dreadful waste and suffering which followed impelled the societies and associations then organized to redoubled effort and induced the formation of new organizations. People everywhere began to realize that their objects were real and not merely sentimental or academic, that they were seeking practical means to remove the conditions which had made the Great War possible. Public opinion became more and more pronounced as the subject was more widely discussed in the journals and periodicals of the day and at public meetings, the divergence of views being chiefly in regard to the means to be employed by the proposed organization and not as to the creation of the organization, the necessity for which appeared to be generally conceded.

With popular sentiment overwhelmingly in favor of some sort of world union which would to an extent insure the nations against another tragedy like the one which in November, 1918, had left the belligerents wasted and exhausted and the whole world a prey to social and industrial unrest, there was beyond question a demand that out of the great international assembly at Paris there should come some common agency devoted to the prevention of war. To ignore this all-prevalent sentiment would have been to misrepresent the peoples of the civilized world and would have aroused almost universal condemnation and protest. The President was, therefore, entirely right in giving prominence to the idea of an international union against war and in insisting that the Peace Conference should make provision for the establishment of an organization of the world with the prevention of future wars as its central thought and purpose.

The great bulk of the American people, at the time that the President left the United States to attend the Peace

Conference, undoubtedly believed that some sort of organization of this nature was necessary, and I am convinced that the same popular belief prevailed in all other civilized countries. It is possible that this assertion may seem too emphatic to some who have opposed the plan for a League of Nations, which appears in the first articles of the Treaty of Versailles, but, if these opponents of the plan will go back to the time of which I am writing, and avoid the impressions made upon them by subsequent events, they will find, I believe, that even their own views have materially changed since December, 1918. It is true that concrete plans had then been suggested, but so far as the public knew the President had not adopted any of them or formulated one of his own. He had not then disclosed the provisions of his "Covenant."

The mass of the people were only concerned with the general idea. There was no well-defined opposition to that idea. At least it was not vocal. Even the defeat of the Democratic Party in the Congressional elections of November, 1918, could not be interpreted to be a repudiation of the formation of a world organization. That election, by which both Houses of Congress became Republican, was a popular rebuke to Mr. Wilson for the partisanship shown in his letter of October addressed to the American people, in which he practically asserted that it was unpatriotic to support the Republican candidates. The indignation and resentment aroused by that injudicious and unwarranted attack upon the loyalty of his political opponents

lost to the Democratic Party the Senate and largely reduced its membership in the House of Representatives if
it did not in fact deprive the party of control of that body.
The result, however, did not mean that the President's
ideas as to the terms of peace were repudiated, but
that his practical assertion, that refusal to accept his
policies was unpatriotic, was repudiated by the American
people.

It is very apparent to one, who without prejudice reviews the state of public sentiment in December, 1918,
that the trouble, which later developed as to a League of
Nations, did not lie in the necessity of convincing the
peoples of the world, their governments, and their delegates to the Paris Conference that it was desirable to organize the world to prevent future wars, but in deciding
upon the form and functions of the organization to be created. As to these details, which of course affected the character, the powers, and the duties of the organization, there
had been for years a wide divergence of opinion. Some
advocated the use of international force to prevent a nation from warring against another. Some favored coercion
by means of general ostracism and non-intercourse. Some
believed that the application of legal justice through the
medium of international tribunals and commissions was
the only practical method of settling disputes which might
become causes of war. And some emphasized the importance of a mutual agreement to postpone actual hostilities until there could be an investigation as to the merits of

a controversy. There were thus two general classes of powers proposed which were in the one case political and in the other juridical. The cleavage of opinion was along these lines, although it possibly was not recognized by the general public. It was not only shown in the proposed powers, but also in the proposed form of the organization, the one centering on a politico-diplomatic body, and the other on an international judiciary. Naturally the details of any plan proposed would become the subject of discussion and the advisability of adopting the provisions would arouse controversy and dispute. Thus unanimity in approving a world organization did not mean that opinions might not differ radically in working out the fundamental principles of its form and functions, to say nothing of the detailed plan based on these principles.

In May, 1916, President Wilson accepted an invitation to address the first annual meeting of the League to Enforce Peace, which was to be held in Washington. After preparing his address he went over it and erased all reference to the use of physical force in preventing wars. I mention this as indicative of the state of uncertainty in which he was in the spring of 1916 as to the functions and powers of the international organization to maintain peace which he then advocated. By January, 1917, he had become convinced that the use of force was the practical method of checking aggressions. This conversion was probably due to the fact that he had in his own mind worked out, as one of the essential bases of peace, to which he was then giving much thought, a mutual guaranty of territorial integrity and political independence, which had been the chief article of a proposed Pan-American Treaty prepared early in 1915 and to which he referred in his address before the League to Enforce Peace. He appears to have reached the conclusion that a guaranty of this sort would be of little value unless supported by the threatened, and, if necessary, the actual, employment of force. The President was entirely logical in this attitude. A guaranty against physical aggression would be practically worthless if it did not rest on an agreement to protect with physical force. An undertaking to protect carried with it the idea of using effectual measures to insure protection. They were inseparable; and the President, having adopted an affirmative guaranty against aggression as a cardinal provision — perhaps I should say *the* cardinal provision — of the anticipated peace treaty, could not avoid becoming the advocate of the use of force in making good the guaranty.

During the year 1918 the general idea of the formation of an international organization to prevent war was increasingly discussed in the press of the United States and Europe and engaged the thought of the Governments of the Powers at war with the German Empire. On January 8 of that year President Wilson in an address to Congress proclaimed his "Fourteen Points," the adoption of which he considered necessary to a just and stable peace. The last of these "Points" explicitly states the basis of the proposed international organization and the fundamental reason for its formation. It is as follows:

"XIV. A general association of nations must be formed under specific covenants for the purpose of affording mutual guarantees of political independence and territorial integrity to great and small states alike."

This declaration may be considered in view of subsequent developments to be a sufficiently clear announcement of the President's theory as to the plan of organization which ought to be adopted, but at the time the exact character of the "mutual guarantees" was not disclosed and aroused little comment. I do not believe that Congress, much less the public at large, understood the purpose that the President had in mind. Undoubtedly, too, a sense of loyalty to the Chief Executive, while the war was in progress, and the desire to avoid giving comfort of any sort to the enemy, prevented a critical discussion of the announced bases of peace, some of which were at the time academic, premature, and liable to modification if conditions changed.

In March Lord Phillimore and his colleagues made their preliminary report to the British Government on "a League of Nations" and this was followed in July by their final report, copies of which reached the President soon after they were made. The time had arrived for putting into concrete form the general ideas that the President held, and Colonel House, whom some believed to be the real author of Mr. Wilson's conception of a world union, prepared, I am informed, the draft of a scheme of organization. This draft was either sent or handed to the President and discussed with him. To what extent it was amended or revised by Mr. Wilson I do not know, but in a modified form it became the typewritten draft of the Covenant which he took with him to Paris, where it underwent several changes. In it was the guaranty of 1915, 1916, 1917, and 1918, which, from the form in which it appeared, logically required the use of force to give it effect.

Previous to the departure of the American Commission for Paris, on December 4, 1918, the President did not consult me as to his plan for a League of Nations. He did not show me a copy of the plan or even mention that one had been put into writing. I think that there were two reasons for his not doing so, although I was the official adviser whom he should naturally consult on such matters.

The first reason, I believe, was due to the following facts. In our conversations prior to 1918 I had uniformly opposed the idea of the employment of international force to compel a nation to respect the rights of other nations and had repeatedly urged judicial settlement as the practical way of composing international controversies, though I did not favor the use of force to compel such settlement.

To show my opposition to an international agreement providing for the use of force and to show that President Wilson knew of this opposition and the reasons for it,

I quote a letter which I wrote to him in May, 1916, that is, two years and a half before the end of the war:

"*May* 25, 1916

"MY DEAR MR. PRESIDENT:

"I had hoped to see you to-morrow at Cabinet meeting, but to-day the Doctor refused to allow me to leave the house this week. I intended when I saw you to say something about the purposes of the League to Enforce Peace, which is to meet here, and at the banquet of which I understand you are to speak on Saturday night. I would have preferred to talk the matter over with you, but as that is impossible I have taken the liberty to write you this letter, although in doing so I am violating the directions of the Doctor.

"While I have not had time or opportunity to study carefully the objects of the proposed League to Enforce Peace, I understand the fundamental ideas are these, which are to be embodied in a general treaty of the nations: *First*, an agreement to submit all differences which fail of diplomatic adjustment to arbitration or a board of conciliation; and, *second*, in case a government fails to comply with this provision, an agreement that the other parties will unite in compelling it to do so by an exercise of force.

"With the first agreement I am in accord to an extent, but I cannot see how it is practicable to apply it in case of a continuing invasion of fundamental national or individual rights unless some authoritative international body has the power to impose and enforce an order in the nature of an injunction, which will prevent the aggressor from further action until arbitration has settled the rights of the parties. How this can be done in a practical way I have not attempted to work out, but the problem is not easy, especially the part which relates to the enforcement of the order.

"It is, however, the second agreement in regard to the imposition of international arbitration by force, which seems to me the most difficult, especially when viewed from the standpoint of its effects on our national sovereignty and national interests. It is needless to go into the manifest questions arising when the *modus operandi* of the agreement is considered. Such questions as: Who may demand international intervention? What body will decide whether the demand should be complied with? How will the international forces be constituted? Who will take charge of the military and naval operations? Who will pay the expenses of the war (for war it will be)?

"Perplexing as these questions appear to me, I am more concerned with the direct effect on this country. I do not believe that it is wise to limit our independence of action, a sovereign right, to the will of other powers beyond this hemisphere. In any representative international body clothed with authority to require of the nations to employ their armies and navies to coerce one of their number, we would be in the minority. I do not believe that we should put ourselves in the position of being compelled to send our armed forces to Europe or Asia or, in the alternative, of repudiating our treaty obligation. Neither our sovereignty nor our interests would accord with such a proposition, and I am convinced that popular opinion as well as the Senate would reject a treaty framed along such lines.

"It is possible that the difficulty might be obviated by the establishment of geographical zones, and leaving to the groups of nations thus formed the enforcement of the peaceful settlement of disputes. But if that is done why should all the world participate? We have adopted a much modified form of this idea in the proposed Pan-American Treaty by the 'guaranty' article. But I would not like to see its stipulations extended to the European powers so that they, with our full agreement, would have the right to cross the ocean and stop quarrels between two American Republics. Such authority would be a serious menace to the Monroe Doctrine and a greater menace to the Pan-American Doctrine.

"It appears to me that, if the first idea of the League can be worked out in a practical way and an international body constituted to determine when steps should be taken to enforce compliance, the use of force might be avoided by outlawing the offending nation. No nation to-day can live unto itself. The industrial and commercial activities of the world are too closely interwoven for a nation isolated from the other nations to thrive and prosper. A tremendous economic pressure could be imposed on the outlawed nation by all other nations denying it intercourse of every nature, even communication, in a word make that nation a pariah, and so to remain until it was willing to perform its obligations.

"I am not at all sure that this means is entirely feasible. I see many difficulties which would have to be met under certain conditions. But I do think that it is more practical in operation and less objectionable from the standpoint of national rights and interests than the one proposed by the League. It does not appear to me that the use of physical force is in any way practical or advisable.

"I presume that you are far more familiar than I am with the details of the plans of the League and that it may be presumptuous on my part to write you as I have. I nevertheless felt it my duty to frankly give you my views on the subject and I have done so.

"Faithfully yours
"ROBERT LANSING

"THE PRESIDENT
  "*The White House*"

The President, thus early advised of my unqualified opposition to any plan which was similar in principle to the one advocated by the League to Enforce Peace, naturally concluded that I would look with disfavor on an international guaranty which by implication, if not by declaration, compelled the use of force to give it effect. Doubtless he felt that I would not be disposed to aid in perfecting a plan which had as its central idea a guaranty of that nature. Disliking opposition to a plan or policy which he had originated or made his own by adoption, he preferred to consult those who without debate accepted his judgment and were in sympathy with his ideas. Undoubtedly the President by refraining from asking my advice spared himself from listening to arguments against the guaranty and the use of force which struck at the very root of his plan, for I should, if I had been asked, have stated my views with entire frankness.

The other reason for not consulting me, as I now realize, but did not at the time, was that I belonged to the legal profession. It is a fact, which Mr. Wilson has taken no trouble to conceal, that he does not value the advice of lawyers except on strictly legal questions, and that he considers their objections and criticisms on other subjects to be too often based on mere technicalities and their judgments to be warped by an undue regard for precedent. This prejudice against the legal profession in general was exhibited on more than one occasion during our sojourn at Paris. Looking back over my years of intercourse with the

President I can now see that he chafed under the restraints imposed by usage and even by enacted laws if they interfered with his acting in a way which seemed to him right or justified by conditions. I do not say that he was lawless. He was not that, but he conformed grudgingly and with manifest displeasure to legal limitations. It was a thankless task to question a proposed course of action on the ground of illegality, because he appeared to be irritated by such an obstacle to his will and to transfer his irritation against the law to the one who raised it as an objection. I think that he was especially resentful toward any one who volunteered criticism based on a legal provision, precept, or precedent, apparently assuming that the critic opposed his purpose on the merits and in order to defeat it interposed needless legal objections. It is unnecessary to comment on the prejudice which such an attitude of mind made evident.

After the President's exceptionally strong address at the Metropolitan Opera House in New York on September 27, 1918, I realized the great importance which he gave to the creation of a League of Nations and in view of this I devoted time and study to the subject, giving particular attention to the British and French suggestions, both of which emphasized judicial settlement. Knowing that the President had been in consultation with Colonel House on the various phases of the peace to be negotiated as well as on the terms of the armistice, I asked the latter what he knew about the former's scheme for a League of Nations.

The Colonel discreetly avoided disclosing the details of the plan, but from our conversation I gained an idea of the general principles of the proposed organization and the way in which the President intended to apply them.

After the Colonel and his party had sailed for France and in expectation of being consulted on the subject by President Wilson, I put my thoughts on the League of Nations into writing. In a note, which is dated October 27, 1918, appears the following:

"From the little I know of the President's plan I am sure that it is impracticable. There is in it too much altruistic coöperation. No account is taken of national selfishness and the mutual suspicions which control international relations. It may be noble thinking, but it is not true thinking.

"What I fear is that a lot of dreamers and theorists will be selected to work out an organization instead of men whose experience and common sense will tell them not to attempt anything which will not work. The scheme ought to be simple and practical. If the federation, or whatever it may be called, is given too much power or if its machinery is complex, my belief is that it will be unable to function or else will be defied. I can see lots of trouble ahead unless impractical enthusiasts and fanatics are suppressed. This is a time when sober thought, caution, and common sense should control."

On November 22, 1918, after I had been formally designated as a Peace Commissioner, I made another note for the purpose of crystallizing my own thought on the subject of a League of Nations. Although President Wilson had not then consulted me in any way regarding his plan of organization, I felt sure that he would, and I wished to be prepared to give him my opinion concerning the fundamentals of the plan which might be proposed on behalf of the United States. I saw, or thought that I saw, a disposition to adopt physical might as the basis of the organization, because the guaranty, which the President had announced in Point XIV and evidently purposed to advocate, seemed to require the use of force in the event that it became necessary to make it good.

From the note of November 22 I quote the following:

"The legal principle [of the equality of nations], whatever its basis in fact, must be preserved, otherwise force rather than law, the power to act rather than the right to act, becomes the fundamental principle of organization, just as it has been in all previous Congresses and Concerts of the European Powers.

"It appears to me that a positive guaranty of territorial integrity and political independence by the nations would have to rest upon an open recognition of dominant coercive power in the articles of agreement, the power being commercial and economic as well as physical. The wisdom of entering into such a guaranty is questionable and should be carefully considered before being adopted.

"In order to avoid the recognition of force as a basis and the question of dominant force with the unavoidable classification of nations into 'big' and 'little,' 'strong' and 'weak,' the desired result of a guaranty might be attained by entering into a mutual undertaking *not* to impair the territorial integrity or to violate the political sovereignty of any state. The breach of this undertaking would be a breach of the treaty and would sever the relations of the offending nation with all other signatories."

I have given these two extracts from my notes in order to show the views that I held, at the time the American Commission was about to depart from the United States, in regard to the character of the guaranty which the President intended to make the central feature of the League of Nations. In the carrying out of his scheme and in creating an organization to give effect to the guaranty I believed that I saw as an unavoidable consequence an exaltation of force and an overlordship of the strong nations. Under such conditions it would be impossible to preserve within the organization the equality of nations, a precept of international law which was the universally recognized basis of intercourse between nations in time of peace. This I considered most unwise and a return to the old order, from which every one hoped that the victory over the Central Empires had freed the world.

The views expressed in the notes quoted formed the basis for my subsequent course of action as an American Commissioner at Paris in relation to the League of Nations. Convinced from previous experience that to oppose every form of guaranty by the nations assembled at Paris would be futile in view of the President's apparent determination to compel the adoption of that principle, I endeavored to find a form of guaranty that would be less objectionable than the one which the President had in mind. The commitment of the United States to any guaranty seemed to me at least questionable, though to prevent it seemed impossible in the circumstances. It did not seem politic to try to persuade the President to abandon the idea altogether. I was certain that that could not be done. If he could be induced to modify his plan so as to avoid a direct undertaking to protect other nations from aggression, the result would be all that could be expected. I was guided, therefore, chiefly by expediency rather than by principle in presenting my views to the President and in openly approving the idea of a guaranty.

The only opportunity that I had to learn more of the President's plan for a League before arriving in Paris was an hour's interview with him on the U.S.S. George Washington some days after we sailed from New York. He showed me nothing in writing, but explained in a general way his views as to the form, purpose, and powers of a League. From this conversation I gathered that my fears as to the proposed organization were justified and that it was to be based on the principle of diplomatic adjustment rather than that of judicial settlement and that political expediency tinctured with morality was to be the standard of determination of an international controversy rather than strict legal justice.

In view of the President's apparent fixity of purpose it seemed unwise to criticize the plan until I could deliver to him a substitute in writing for the mutual guaranty which he evidently considered to be the chief feature of the plan. I did not attempt to debate the subject with him believing it better to submit my ideas in concrete form, as I had learned from experience that Mr. Wilson preferred to have matters for his decision presented in writing rather than by word of mouth.

CHAPTER IV
SUBSTITUTE ARTICLES PROPOSED

THE President, Mr. Henry White, and I arrived in Paris on Saturday, December 14, 1918, where Colonel House and General Bliss awaited us. The days following our arrival were given over to public functions in honor of the President and to official exchanges of calls and interviews with the delegates of other countries who were gathering for the Peace Conference. On the 23d, when the pressure of formal and social engagements had in a measure lessened, I decided to present to the President my views as to the mutual guaranty which he intended to propose, fearing that, if there were further delay, he would become absolutely committed to the affirmative form. I, therefore, on that day sent him the following letter, which was marked "Secret and Urgent":

"*Hôtel de Crillon*
December 23, 1918

"MY DEAR MR. PRESIDENT:

"The plan of guaranty proposed for the League of Nations, which has been the subject of discussion, will find considerable objection from other Governments because, even when the principle is agreed to, there will be a wide divergence of views as to the terms of the obligation. This difference of opinion will be seized upon by those, who are openly or secretly opposed to the League, to create controversy and discord.

THE RUE ROYALE ON THE ARRIVAL OF PRESIDENT WILSON
DECEMBER 14, 1918

"In addition to this there will be opposition in Congress to assuming obligations to take affirmative action along either military or economic lines. On constitutional grounds, on its effect on the Monroe Doctrine, on jealousy as to Congressional powers, etc., there will be severe criticism which will materially weaken our position with other nations, and may, in view of senatorial hostility, defeat a treaty as to the League of Nations or at least render it impotent.

"With these thoughts in mind and with an opposition known to exist among certain European statesmen and already manifest in Washington, I take the liberty of laying before you a tentative draft of articles of guaranty which I do not believe can be successfully opposed either at home or abroad."

I would interrupt the reader at this point to suggest that it might be well to peruse the enclosures, which will be found in the succeeding pages, in order to have a better understanding of the comments which follow. To continue:

"I do not see how any nation can refuse to subscribe to them. I do not see how any question of constitutionality can be raised, as they are based essentially on powers which are confided to the Executive. They in no way raise a question as to the Monroe Doctrine. At the same time I believe that the result would be as efficacious as if there was an undertaking to take positive action against an offending nation, which is the present cause of controversy.

"I am so earnestly in favor of the guaranty, which is the heart of the League of Nations, that I have endeavored to find a way to accomplish this and to remove the objections raised which seem to me to-day to jeopardize the whole plan.

"I shall be glad, if you desire it, to confer with you in regard to the enclosed paper or to receive your opinion as to the suggestions made. In any event it is my hope that you will give the paper consideration.

"Faithfully yours

"ROBERT LANSING

"THE PRESIDENT
    "28 *Rue de Monceau*"

It should be borne in mind in reading this letter that I had reached the conclusion that modification rather than abandonment of the guaranty was all that I could hope to accomplish, and that, as a matter of expediency, it seemed wise to indicate a sympathetic attitude toward the idea. For that reason I expressed myself as favorable to the guaranty and termed it "the heart of the League of Nations," a phrase which the President by his subsequent use of it considered to be a proper characterization.

The memoranda contained in the paper enclosed in the letter were as follows:

The Constitutional Power to provide Coercion in a Treaty

"*December* 20, 1918

"In the institution of a League of Nations we must bear in mind the limitations imposed by the Constitution of the United States upon the Executive and Legislative Branches of the Government in defining their respective powers.

"The Constitution confers upon Congress the right to declare war. This right, I do not believe, can be delegated and it certainly cannot be taken away by treaty. The question arises, therefore, as to how far a provision in an agreement as to a League of Nations, which imposes on the United States the obligation to employ its military or naval forces in enforcing the terms of the agreement, would be constitutional.

"It would seem that the utilization of forces, whether independently or in conjunction with other nations, would in fact by being an act of war create a state of war, which constitutionally can only be done by a declaration of Congress. To contract by treaty to create a state of war upon certain contingencies arising would be equally tainted with unconstitutionality and would be null and inoperative.

"I do not think, therefore, that, even if it were advisable, any treaty can provide for the independent or joint use of the military or naval forces of the United States to compel compliance with a treaty or to make good a guaranty made in a treaty.

"The other method of international coercion is non-intercourse, especially commercial non-intercourse. Would a treaty provision to employ this method be constitutional?

"As to this my mind is less clear. The Constitution in delegating powers to Congress includes the regulation of commerce. Does non-intercourse fall within the idea of regulation? Could an embargo be imposed without an act of Congress? My impression is that it could not be done without legislation and that a treaty provision agreeing in a certain event to impose an embargo against another nation would be void.

"Even if Congress was willing to delegate to the Executive for a certain purpose its powers as to making war and regulating commerce, I do not think that it could constitutionally do so. It is only in the event of war that powers conferred by the Constitution on Congress can be delegated and then only for war purposes. As a state of war would not exist at the time action was required, I do not believe that it could be done, and any provision contracting to take measures of this nature would be contrary to the Constitution and as a consequence void.

"But, assuming that Congress possessed the power of delegation, I am convinced that it would not only refuse to do so, but would resent such a suggestion because of the fact that both Houses have been and are extremely jealous of their rights and authority.

"Viewed from the standpoints of legality and expediency it would seem necessary to find some other method than coercion in enforcing an international guaranty, or else to find some substitute for a guaranty which would be valueless without affirmative action to support it.

"I believe that such a substitute can be found."

The foregoing memorandum was intended as an introduction to the negative guaranty or "self-denying covenant" which I desired to lay before the President as a substitute for the one upon which he intended to build the League of Nations. The memorandum was suggestive merely, but in view of the necessity for a speedy decision there was no time to prepare an exhaustive legal opinion. Furthermore, I felt that the President, whose hours were at that time crowded with numerous personal conferences and public functions, would find little opportunity to peruse a long and closely reasoned argument on the subject.

The most important portion of the document was that

entitled "*Suggested Draft of Articles for Discussion.* December 20, 1918." It reads as follows:

"The parties to this convention, for the purpose of maintaining international peace and preventing future wars between one another, hereby constitute themselves into a League of Nations and solemnly undertake jointly and severally to fulfill the obligations imposed upon them in the following articles:

"A

"Each power signatory or adherent hereto severally covenants and guarantees that it will not violate the territorial integrity or impair the political independence of any other power signatory or adherent to this convention except when authorized so to do by a decree of the arbitral tribunal hereinafter referred to or by a three-fourths vote of the International Council of the League of Nations created by this convention.

"B

"In the event that any power signatory or adherent hereto shall fail to observe the covenant and guaranty set forth in the preceding article, such breach of covenant and guaranty shall *ipso facto* operate as an abrogation of this convention in so far as it applies to the offending power and furthermore as an abrogation of all treaties, conventions, and agreements heretofore or hereafter entered into between the offending power and all other powers signatory and adherent to this convention.

"C

"A breach of the covenant and guaranty declared in Article A shall constitute an act unfriendly to all other powers signatory and adherent hereto, and they shall forthwith sever all diplomatic, consular, and official relations with the offending power, and shall, through the International Council, hereinafter provided for, exchange views as to the measures necessary to restore the power, whose sovereignty has been invaded, to the rights and liberties which it possessed prior to such invasion and to prevent further violation thereof.

"D

"Any interference with a vessel on the high seas or with aircraft proceeding over the high seas, which interference is not affirmatively sanctioned by the law of nations shall be, for the purposes of this convention, considered an impairment of political independence."

In considering the foregoing series of articles constituting a guaranty against one's own acts, instead of a guaranty against the acts of another, it must be remembered that, at the time of their preparation, I had not seen a draft of the President's proposed guaranty, though from conversations with Colonel House and from my study of Point XIV of "The Fourteen Points," I knew that it was affirmative rather than negative in form and would require positive action to be effective in the event that the menace of superior force was insufficient to prevent aggressive acts.

As far as I am able to judge from subsequently acquired knowledge, President Wilson at the time he received my letter of December 23 had a typewritten draft of the document which after certain amendments he later laid before the American Commissioners and which he had printed with a few verbal changes under the title of "The Covenant." In order to understand the two forms of guaranty which he had for consideration after he received my letter, I quote the article relating to it, which appears in the first printed draft of the Covenant.

"III

"The Contracting Powers unite in guaranteeing to each other political independence and territorial integrity; but it is understood between them that such territorial readjustments, if any, as may in the future become necessary by reasons of changes in present racial conditions and aspirations or present social and political relationships, pursuant to the principle of self-determination, and also such territorial readjustments as may in the judgment of three fourths of the Delegates be demanded by the welfare and manifest interest of the people concerned, may be effected if agreeable to those peoples; and that territorial changes may involve material compensation. The Contracting Powers accept without reservation the principle that the peace of the world is superior in importance to every question of political jurisdiction or boundary."

It seems needless to comment upon the involved language and the uncertainty of meaning of this article wherein it provided for "territorial readjustments" of which there appeared to be two classes, one dependent on "self-determination," the other on the judgment of the Body of Delegates of the League. In view of the possible reasons which might be advanced for changes in territory and allegiance, justification for an appeal to the guarantors was by no means certain. If this article had been before me when the letter of December 23 was written, I might have gone much further in opposition to the President's plan for stabilizing peace in the world on the ground that a guaranty so conditioned would cause rather than prevent international discord.

Though without knowledge of the exact terms of the President's proposed guaranty, I did not feel for the reason stated that I could delay longer in submitting my views to the President. There was not time to work out a complete and well-digested plan for a League, but I had prepared in the rough several articles for discussion which related to the organization, and which might be incorporated in the organic agreement which I then assumed would be a separate document from the treaty restoring peace. While unwilling to lay these articles before the President until they were more carefully drafted, I enclosed in my letter the following as indicative of the character of the organization which it seemed to me would form a simple and practical agency common to all nations:

" *Suggestions as to an International Council*
"*For Discussion*

"*December* 21, 1918

"An International Council of the League of Nations is hereby constituted, which shall be the channel for communication between the members of the League, and the agent for common action.

"The International Council shall consist of the diplomatic representative of each party signatory or adherent to this convention at ———.

"Meetings of the International Council shall be held at ———, or in the event that the subject to be considered involves the interests of ——— or its nationals, then at such other place outside the territory of a power whose interests are involved as the Supervisory Committee of the Council shall designate.

"The officer charged with the conduct of the foreign affairs of the power where a meeting is held shall be the presiding officer thereof.

"At the first meeting of the International Council a Supervisory Committee shall be chosen by a majority vote of the members present, which shall consist of five members and shall remain in office for two years or until their successors are elected.

"The Supervisory Committee shall name a Secretariat which shall have charge of the archives of the Council and receive all communications addressed to the Council or Committee and send all communications issued by the Council or Committee.

"The Supervisory Committee may draft such rules of procedure as it deems necessary for conducting business coming before the Council or before the Committee.

"The Supervisory Committee may call a meeting of the Council at its discretion and must call a meeting at the request of any member of the Council provided the request contains a written statement of the subject to be discussed.

"The archives of the Council shall be open at any time to any member of the Council, who may make and retain copies thereof.

"All expenses of the Supervisory Committee and Secretariat shall be borne equally by all powers signatory or adherent to this convention."

As indicated by the caption, this document was intended merely "for discussion" of the principal features of the organization. It should be noted that the basic principle is the equality of nations. No special privileges are granted to the major powers in the conduct of the organization. The rights and obligations of one member of the League are no more and no less than those of every other member. It is based on international democracy and denies international aristocracy.

Equality in the exercise of sovereign rights in times of peace, an equality which is imposed by the very nature of sovereignty, seemed to me fundamental to a world organization affecting in any way a nation's independence of action or its exercise of supreme authority over its external or domestic affairs. In my judgment any departure from that principle would be a serious error fraught with danger to the general peace of the world and to the recognized law of nations, since it could mean nothing less than the primacy of the Great Powers and the acknowledgment that because they possessed the physical might they had a right to control the affairs of the world in times of peace as well as in times of war. For the United States to admit that such a primacy ought to be formed would be bad enough, but to suggest it indirectly by proposing an international organization based on that idea would be far worse.

On January 22, 1917, the President in an address to the Senate had made the following declaration:

"The equality of nations upon which peace must be founded if it is to last must be an equality of rights; the guarantees exchanged must neither recognize nor imply a difference between big nations or small, between those that are powerful and those that are weak. Right must be based upon the common strength, not the individual strength, of the nations upon whose concert peace will depend. Equality of territory or of resources there of course cannot be; nor any other sort of equality not gained in the ordinary peaceful and legitimate development of the peoples themselves. But no one asks or expects anything more than an equality of rights."

In view of this sound declaration of principle it seemed hardly possible that the President, after careful consideration of the consequences of his plan of a guaranty requiring force to make it practical, would not perceive the fundamental error of creating a primacy of the Great Powers.

It was in order to prevent, if possible, the United States from becoming sponsor for an undemocratic principle that I determined to lay my partial plan of organization before the President at the earliest moment that I believed it would receive consideration.

To my letter of December 23 with its enclosed memoranda I never received a reply or even an acknowledgment. It is true that the day following its delivery the President went to Chaumont to spend Christmas at the headquarters of General Pershing and that almost immediately thereafter he visited London and two or three days after his return to Paris he set out for Rome. It is possible that Mr. Wilson in the midst of these crowded days had no time to digest or even to read my letter and its enclosed memoranda. It is possible that he was unable or unwilling to form an opinion as to their merits without time for meditation. I do not wish to be unjustly critical or to blame the President for a neglect which was the result of circumstance rather than of intention.

At the time I assumed that his failure to mention my letter in any way was because his visits to royalty exacted from him so much of his time that there was no opportunity to give the matter consideration. While some doubt was thrown on this assumption by the fact that the President held an hour's conference with the American Commissioners on January 1, just before departing for Italy, during which he discussed the favorable attitude of Mr. Lloyd George toward his (the President's) ideas as to a League of Nations, but never made any reference to my proposed substitute for the guaranty, I was still disposed to believe that there was a reasonable explanation for his silence and that upon his return from Rome he would discuss it.

Having this expectation I continued the preparation of tentative provisions to be included in the charter of a League of Nations in the event one was negotiated, and which would in any event constitute a guide for the prepa-

ration of declarations to be included in the Treaty of
Peace in case the negotiation as to a League was postponed until after peace had been restored. As has been
said, it was my hope that there would be a separate convention organizing the League, but I was not as sanguine of
this as many who believed this course would be followed.

It later developed that the President never had any
other purpose than to include the detailed plan of organization in the peace treaty, whether the treaty was preliminary or definitive. When he departed for Italy he had
not declared this purpose to the Commissioners, but from
some source, which I failed to note at the time and cannot
now recollect, I gained the impression that he intended to
pursue this policy, for on December 29 I wrote in my book
of notes:

"It is evident that the President is determined to incorporate in the peace treaty an elaborate scheme for the
League of Nations which will excite all sorts of opposition
at home and abroad and invite much discussion.

"The articles relating to the League ought to be few and
brief. They will not be. They will be many and long. If
we wait till they are accepted, it will be four or five months
before peace is signed, and I fear to say how much longer
it will take to have it ratified.

"It is perhaps foolish to prophesy, but I will take the
chance. Two months from now we will still be haggling
over the League of Nations and an exasperated world will
be cursing us for not having made peace. I hope that I am
a false prophet, but I fear my prophecy will come true.
We are riding a hobby, and riding to a fall."

By the time the President returned from his triumphal journey to Rome I had completed the articles upon which I had been working; at least they were in form for discussion. At a conference at the Hôtel Crillon between President Wilson and the American Commissioners on January 7, I handed to him the draft articles saying that they were supplemental to my letter of December 23. He took them without comment and without making any reference to my unanswered letter.

The first two articles of the "International Agreement," as I termed the document, were identical in language with the memoranda dealing with a mutual covenant and with an international council which I had enclosed in my letter of December 23. It is needless, therefore, to repeat them here.

Article III of the so-called "Agreement" was entitled "Peaceful Settlements of International Disputes," and read as follows:

"*Clause* 1

"In the event that there is a controversy between two or more members of the League of Nations which fails of settlement through diplomatic channels, one of the following means of settlement shall be employed:

"1. The parties to the controversy shall constitute a joint commission to investigate and report jointly or severally to their Governments the facts and make recommendations as to settlement. After such report a further effort shall be made to reach a diplomatic settlement of the controversy.

"2. The parties shall by agreement arrange for the submission of the controversy to arbitration mutually agreed upon, or to the Arbitral Tribunal hereinafter referred to.

"3. Any party may, unless the second means of settlement is mutually adopted, submit the controversy to the Supervisory Committee of the International Council; and the Committee shall forthwith (a) name and direct a special commission to investigate and report upon the subject; (b) name and direct a commission to mediate between the parties to the controversy; or (c) direct the parties to submit the controversy to the Arbitral Tribunal for judicial settlement, it being understood that the direction to arbitrate may be made at any time in the event that investigation and mediation fail to result in a settlement of the controversy.

"*Clause 2*

"No party to a controversy shall assume any authority or perform any acts based upon disputed rights without authorization of the Supervisory Committee, such authorization being limited in all cases to the pendency of the controversy and its final settlement and being in no way prejudicial to the rights of the parties. An authorization thus granted by the Supervisory Committee may be modified or superseded by mutual agreement of the parties, by order of an arbitrator or arbitrators selected by the parties, or by order of the Arbitral Tribunal if the controversy is submitted to it.

"*Clause 3*

"The foregoing clause shall not apply to cases in which the constituted authorities of a power are unable or fail to give protection to the lives and property of nationals of another power. In the event that it becomes necessary for a power to use its military or naval forces to safeguard the lives or property of its nationals within the territorial jurisdiction of another power, the facts and reasons for such action shall be forthwith reported to the Supervisory Committee, which shall determine the course of action to be adopted in order to protect the rights of all parties, and shall notify the same to the governments involved which shall comply with such notification. In the event that a government fails to comply therewith it shall be deemed to have violated the covenant and guaranty hereinbefore set forth."

The other articles follow:

"ARTICLE IV

"Revision of Arbitral Tribunal and Codification of International Law

"Clause 1

"The International Council, within one year after its organization, shall notify to the powers signatory and adherent to this convention and shall invite all other powers to send delegates to an international conference at such place and time as the Council may determine and not later than six months after issuance of such notification and invitation.

"Clause 2

"The International Conference shall consider the revision of the constitution and procedure of the Arbitral Tribunal and provisions for the amicable settlement of international disputes established by the I Treaty signed at The Hague in 1907, and shall formulate codes embodying the principles of international law applicable in time of peace and the rules of warfare on land and sea and in the air. The revision and codification when completed shall be embodied in a treaty or treaties.

"*Clause* 3

"The International Council shall prepare and submit with the notification and invitation above provided a preliminary programme of the International Conference, which shall be subject to modification or amendment by the Conference.

"*Clause* 4

"Until the treaty of revision of the constitution and procedure of the Arbitral Tribunal becomes operative, the provisions of the I Treaty signed at The Hague in 1907 shall continue in force, and all references herein to the 'Arbitral Tribunal' shall be understood to be the Tribunal constituted under the I Treaty, but upon the treaty of revision coming into force the references shall be construed as applying to the Arbitral Tribunal therein constituted.

"ARTICLE V

"*Publication of Treaties and Agreements*

"*Clause* 1

"Each power, signatory or adherent to this convention, severally agrees with all other parties hereto that it will not exchange the ratification of any treaty or convention hereinafter entered into by it with any other power until thirty days after the full text of such treaty or convention has been published in the public press of the parties thereto and a copy has been filed with the Secretariat of the League of Nations.

"*Clause* 2

"No international agreement, to which a power signatory or adherent to this convention, is a party, shall become operative or be put in force until published and filed as aforesaid.

"*Clause* 3

"All treaties, conventions and agreements, to which a power, signatory or adherent to this convention, is a party, and which are in force or to come into force and which have not been heretofore published, shall within six months after the signature of this convention be published and filed as aforesaid or abrogated or denounced.

"ARTICLE VI

"*Equality of Commercial Privileges*

"The powers, signatory and adherent to this convention agree jointly and severally not to discriminate against or in favor of any power in the matter of commerce or trade or of industrial privileges; and they further agree that all treaties, conventions and agreements now in force or to come into force or hereinafter negotiated shall be considered as subject to the 'most favored nation' doctrine, whether they contain or do not contain a clause to that effect. It is specifically declared that it is the purpose of this article not to limit any power in imposing upon commerce and trade such restrictions and burdens as it may deem proper but to make such impositions apply equally and impartially to all other powers, their nationals and ships.

"This article shall not apply, however, to any case, in which a power has committed an unfriendly act against the members of the League of Nations as defined in Article I and in which commercial and trade relations are denied or restricted by agreements between the members as a measure of restoration or protection of the rights of a power injured by such unfriendly act."

These proposed articles, which were intended for discussion before drafting the provisions constituting a League of Nations and which did not purport to be a completed document, are given in full because there seems no simpler method of showing the differences between the President and me as to the form, functions, and authority of an international organization. They should be compared with the draft of the "Covenant" which the President had when these proposed articles were handed to him; the text of the President's draft appears in the Appendix (page 281). Comparison will disclose the irreconcilable differences between the two projects.

Of these differences the most vital was in the character of the international guaranty of territorial and political sovereignty. That difference has already been discussed. The second in importance was the practical repudiation by the President of the doctrine of the equality of nations, which, as has been shown, was an unavoidable consequence of an affirmative guaranty which he had declared to be absolutely essential to an effective world union. The repudiation, though by indirection, was none the less evident in the recognition in the President's plan of the primacy of the Great Powers through giving to them a permanent majority on the "Executive Council" which body substantially controlled the activities of the League. A third marked difference was in Mr. Wilson's exaltation of the executive power of the League and the subordination of the administration of legal justice to that power, and in my advocacy of an independent international judiciary, whose decisions would be final and whose place in the organization of the nations would be superior, since I considered a judicial tribunal the most practical agency for removing causes of war.

The difference as to international courts and the importance of applied legal justice requires further consideration in order to understand the divergence of views which existed as to the fundamental idea of organization of the League.

President Wilson in his Covenant, as at first submitted to the American Commissioners, made no provision for the establishment of a World Court of Justice, and no reference of any sort was made to The Hague Tribunal of Arbitration. It is not, in my opinion, a misstatement to say that the President intentionally omitted judicial means of composing international disputes preferring to leave settlements of that sort to arrangement between the parties or else to the Body of Delegates or the Executive Council, both of which bodies being essentially diplomatic or political in their composition would lack the judicial point of view, since their members would presumably be influenced by their respective national interests and by political considerations rather than by a desire and purpose to do impartial justice by applying legal principles.

It is true that in Article V of the first draft of the Covenant (Appendix, page 285) there is an agreement to submit to arbitration certain classes of controversies and a method of selecting arbitrators is provided — a method, by the way, which the actual experience of a century has shown to be the least satisfactory in administering legal justice, since it almost inevitably leads to a compromise which impairs the just rights of one of the parties. But, to my mind, a provision, far more objectionable than the antiquated and unsatisfactory method of arbitration provided, was that which made an arbitral award reviewable on appeal to the Body of Delegates of the League, which could set aside the award even if the arbitrators had rendered a unanimous decision and compel a rehearing before other arbitrators. International arbitration as a method of applying the principles of justice to disputes between nations would, in the first instance at least, have become a farce if this provision had been adopted. As an award based on compromise is seldom, if ever, satisfactory to both parties, the right of appeal would in substantially every case have been invoked and the award would have been reviewed by the Body of Delegates, who would practically render a final decision since the new arbitrators would presumably adopt it. The effect of this provision as to appeals was, therefore, to supplant judicial settlements by political compromises and diplomatic adjustments, in which the national interests of the judges, many of whom would be untrained in juridical procedure, would be decided, if not deciding, factors. Manifestly the expediency of the moment would be far more potent in the decisions reached than the principles and precepts of international law.

I shall not express here my opinion as to the reasons which I believe impelled the President to insert in the Covenant these extraordinary provisions which deprived arbitral courts of that independence of the executive authority which has been in modern times considered essential to the impartial administration of justice. But, when one considers how jealously and effectively the Constitution of the United States and the constitutions of the various States of the Union guard the judiciary from executive and legislative interference, the proposal in the President's plan for a League of Nations to abandon that great principle in the settlement of international disputes of a justiciable nature causes speculation as to Mr. Wilson's real opinion of the American political system which emphasizes the separation and independence of the three coördinate branches of government.

That a provision found its way into the draft of the Covenant, which the President, on February 3, 1919, laid before the Commission on the League of Nations, declaring for the creation by the League of a permanent court of international justice, was not due, I feel sure, to any spontaneous thought on the part of President Wilson.

My own views as to the relative value of the settlement of an international controversy, which is by its nature justiciable, by a body of diplomats and of the settlement by a body of trained jurists were fully set forth in an address which I delivered before the American Bar Association at its annual meeting at Boston on September 5, 1919.

An extract from that address will show the radical difference between the President's views and mine.

"While abstract justice cannot [under present conditions] be depended upon as a firm basis on which to constitute an international concord for the preservation of peace and good relations between nations, legal justice offers a common ground where the nations can meet to settle their controversies. No nation can refuse in the face of the opinion of the world to declare its unwillingness to recognize the legal rights of other nations or to submit to the judgment of an impartial tribunal a dispute involving the determination of such rights. The moment, however, that we go beyond the clearly defined field of legal justice we enter the field of diplomacy where national interests and ambitions are to-day the controlling factors of national action. Concession and compromise are the chief agents of diplomatic settlement instead of the impartial application of legal justice which is essential to a judicial settlement. Furthermore, the two modes of settlement differ in that a judicial settlement rests upon the precept that all nations, whether great or small, are equal, but in the sphere of diplomacy the inequality of nations is not only recognized, but unquestionably influences the adjustment of international differences. Any change in the relative power of nations, a change which is continually taking place, makes more or less temporary diplomatic settlements, but in no way affects a judicial settlement.

"However, then, international society may be organized for the future and whatever machinery may be set up to minimize the possibilities of war, I believe that the agency which may be counted upon to function with certainty is that which develops and applies legal justice.

Every other agency, regardless of its form, will be found, when analyzed, to be diplomatic in character and subject to those impulses and purposes which generally affect diplomatic negotiations. With a full appreciation of the advantage to be gained for the world at large through the common consideration of a vexatious international question by a body representing all nations, we ought not to lose sight of the fact that such consideration and the action resulting from it are essentially diplomatic in nature. It is, in brief, the transference of a dispute in a particular case from the capitals of the disputants to the place where the delegates of the nations assemble to deliberate together on matters which affect their common interests. It does not — and this we should understand — remove the question from the processes of diplomacy or prevent the influences which enter into diplomacy from affecting its consideration. Nor does it to an appreciable extent change the actual inequality which exists among nations in the matter of power and influence.

"On the other hand, justice applied through the agency of an impartial tribunal clothed with an international jurisdiction eliminates the diplomatic methods of compromise and concession and recognizes that before the law all nations are equal and equally entitled to the exercise of their rights as sovereign and independent states. In a word, international democracy exists in the sphere of legal justice and, up to the present time, in no other relation between nations.

"Let us, then, with as little delay as possible establish an international tribunal or tribunals of justice with The Hague Court as a foundation; let us provide an easier, a cheaper, and better procedure than now exists; and let us draft a simple and concise body of legal principles to be applied to the questions to be adjudicated. When that has been accomplished — and it ought not to be a difficult task if the delegates of the Governments charged with it are chosen for their experience and learning in the field of jurisprudence — we shall, in my judgment, have done more to prevent international wars through removing their causes than can be done by any other means that has been devised or suggested."

The views, which I thus publicly expressed at Boston in September, 1919, while the President was upon his tour of the country in favor of the Covenant of the League of Nations, were the same as those that I held at Paris in December, 1918, before I had seen the President's first draft of a Covenant, as the following will indicate.

On December 17, 1918, three days after arriving in Paris, I had, as has been stated, a long conference with Colonel House on the Peace Conference and the subjects to come before it. I urged him in the course of our conversation "to persuade the President to make the nucleus of his proposed League of Nations an international court pointing out that it was the simplest and best way of organizing the world for peace, and that, if in addition the general principles of international law were codified and the right of inquiry confided to the court, everything practical would have been done to prevent wars in the future" (quoted from a memorandum of the conversation made at the time). I also urged upon the Colonel that The Hague Tribunal be made the basis of the judicial organization, but that it be expanded and improved to meet the new conditions. I shall have something further to say on this subject.

Reverting now to the draft of articles which I had in form on January 5, 1919, it must be borne in mind that I then had no reason to think that the President would omit from his plan an independent judicial agency for the administration of legal justice, although I did realize that he gave first place to the mutual guaranty and intended to build a League on that as a nucleus. It did not seem probable that an American, a student of the political institutions of the United States and familiar with their operation, would fail to incorporate in any scheme for world organization a judicial system which would be free from the control and even from the influence of the political and diplomatic branch of the organization. The benefit, if not the necessity, of such a division of authority seemed so patent that the omission of a provision to that effect in the original draft of the Covenant condemned it to one who believed in the principles of government which found expression in American institutions. Fortunately the defect was in a measure cured before the Commission on the League of Nations formally met to discuss the subject, though not before the Covenant had been laid before the American Commissioners.

The articles of a proposed convention for the creation of an international organization were not intended, as I have said, to form a complete convention. They were suggestive only of the principal features of a plan which could, if the President desired, arouse discussion as to the right theory and the fundamental principles of the international organization which there seemed little doubt would be declared by the Paris Conference.

Among the suggested articles there was none covering the subject of disarmament, because the problem was highly technical requiring the consideration of military and naval experts. Nor was there any reference to the mandatory system because there had not been, to my knowledge, any mention of it at that time in connection with the President's plan, though General Smuts had given it prominence in his proposed scheme.

During the preparation of these suggestive articles I made a brief memorandum on the features, which seemed to me salient, of any international agreement to prevent wars in the future, and which in my opinion ought to be in mind when drafting such an agreement. The first three paragraphs of the memorandum follow:

"There are three doctrines which should be incorporated in the Treaty of Peace if wars are to be avoided and equal justice is to prevail in international affairs.

"These three doctrines may be popularly termed 'Hands Off,' the 'Open Door,' and 'Publicity.'

"The first pertains to national possessions and national rights; the second to international commerce and economic conditions; and the third, to international agreements."

An examination of the articles which I prepared shows that these doctrines are developed in them, although at the time I was uncertain whether they ought to appear in the convention creating the League or in the Preliminary Treaty of Peace, which I believed, in common with the prevailing belief, would be negotiated. My impression was that they should appear in the Peace Treaty and possibly be repeated in the League Treaty, if the two were kept distinct.

CHAPTER V

THE AFFIRMATIVE GUARANTY AND BALANCE OF POWER

WHILE I was engaged in the preparation of these articles for discussion, which were based primarily on the equality of nations and avoided a mutual guaranty or other undertaking necessitating a departure from that principle, M. Clemenceau delivered an important address in the Chamber of Deputies at its session on December 30, 1918. In this address the French Premier declared himself in favor of maintaining the doctrine of "the balance of power" and of supporting it by a concert of the Great Powers. During his remarks he made the following significant assertion, "This system of alliances, which I do not renounce, will be my guiding thought at the Conference, if your confidence sends me to it, so that there will be no separation in peace of the four powers which have battled side by side."

M. Clemenceau's words caused a decided sensation among the delegates already in Paris and excited much comment in the press. The public interest was intensified by the fact that President Wilson had but a day or two before, in an address at Manchester, England, denounced the doctrine of "the balance of power" as belonging to the old international order which had been repudiated because it had produced the conditions that resulted in the Great War.

A week after the delivery of M. Clemenceau's address I discussed his declarations at some length with Colonel House, and he agreed with me that the doctrine was entirely contrary to the public opinion of the world and that every effort should be made to prevent its revival and to end the "system of alliances" which M. Clemenceau desired to continue.

During this conversation I pointed out that the form of affirmative guaranty, which the President then had in mind, would unavoidably impose the burden of enforcing it upon the Great Powers, and that they, having that responsibility, would demand the right to decide at what time and in what manner the guaranty should be enforced. This seemed to me to be only a different application of the principle expressed in the doctrine of "the balance of power" and to amount to a practical continuance of the alliances formed for prosecution of the war. I said that, in my judgment, if the President's guaranty was made the central idea of the League of Nations, it would play directly into the hands of M. Clemenceau because it could mean nothing other than the primacy of the great military and naval powers; that I could not understand how the President was able to harmonize his plan of a positive guaranty with his utterances at Manchester; and that, if he clung to his plan, he would have to accept the Clemenceau doctrine, which would to all intents transform the

Conference into a second Congress of Vienna and result in a reversion to the old undesirable order, and its continuance in the League of Nations.

It was my hope that Colonel House, to whom I had shown the letter and memoranda which I had sent to the President, would be so impressed with the inconsistency of favoring the affirmative guaranty and of opposing the doctrine of "the balance of power," that he would exert his influence with the President to persuade him to find a substitute for the guaranty which Mr. Wilson then favored. It seemed politic to approach the President in this way in view of the fact that he had never acknowledged my letter or manifested any inclination to discuss the subject with me.

This hope was increased when the Colonel came to me on the evening of the same day that we had the conversation related above and told me that he was "entirely converted" to my plan for a negative guaranty and for the organization of a League.

At this second interview Colonel House gave me a typewritten copy of the President's plan and asked me to examine it and to suggest a way to amend it so that it would harmonize with my views. This was the first time that I had seen the President's complete plan for a League. My previous knowledge had been gained orally and was general and more or less vague in character except as to the guaranty of which I had an accurate idea through the President's "Bases of Peace" of 1917, and Point XIV of his address of January 8, 1918. At the time that the type-written plan was handed to me another copy had already been given to the printer of the Commission. It was evident, therefore, that the President was satisfied with the document. It contained the theory and fundamental principles which he advocated for world organization.

CHAPTER VI

THE PRESIDENT'S PLAN AND THE CECIL PLAN

I IMMEDIATELY began an examination and analysis of the President's plan for a League, having in mind Colonel House's suggestion that I consider a way to modify it so that it would harmonize with my views. The more I studied the document, the less I liked it. A cursory reading of the plan, which is printed in the Appendix (page 281), will disclose the looseness of the language and the doubtful interpretation of many of the provisions. It showed an inexpertness in drafting and a fault in expression which were chargeable to lack of appreciation of the need of exactness or else to haste in preparation. This fault in the paper, which was very apparent, could, however, be cured and was by no means a fatal defect. As a matter of fact, the faults of expression were to a certain extent removed by subsequent revisions, though some of the vagueness and ambiguity of the first draft persisted and appeared in the final text of the Covenant.

The more serious defects of the plan were in the principles on which it was based and in their application under the provisions of the articles proposed. The contemplated use of force in making good the guaranty of sovereign rights and the establishment of a primacy of the Great Powers were provided for in language which was sufficiently explicit to admit of no denial. In my opinion these provisions were entirely out of harmony with American ideals, policies, and traditions. Furthermore, the clauses in regard to arbitration and appeals from arbitral awards, to which reference has been made, the lack of any provision for the establishment of a permanent international judiciary, and the introduction of the mandatory system were strong reasons to reject the President's plan.

It should be borne in mind that, at the time that this document was placed in my hands, the plan of General Smuts for a League of Nations had, as I have said, been printed in the press and in pamphlet form and had been given wide publicity. In the Smuts plan, which gave first place to the system of mandates, appeared the declaration that the League of Nations was to acquire the mandated territories as "the heir of the Empires." This clever and attractive phrase caught the fancy of the President, as was evident from his frequent repetition and approval of it in discussing mandates under the League. Just as General Smuts had adopted the President's "self-determination," Mr. Wilson seized upon the Smuts idea with avidity and incorporated it in his plan. It unquestionably had a decided influence upon his conception of the right way to dispose of the colonial possessions of Germany and of the proper relation of the newly created European states to the League of Nations. As an example of the way in which President Wilson understood and applied General Smuts's phrase to the new states, I quote the following from the

"Supplementary Agreements" forming part of the first printed draft of the President's Covenant, but which I believe were added to the typewritten draft after the President had examined the plan of the South African statesman:

"As successor to the Empires, the League of Nations is empowered, directly and without right of delegation, to watch over the relations *inter se* of all new independent states arising or created out of the Empires, and shall assume and fulfill the duty of conciliating and composing differences between them with a view to the maintenance of settled order and the general peace."

There is a natural temptation to a student of international agreements to analyze critically the composition and language of this provision, but to do so would in no way advance the consideration of the subject under discussion and would probably be interpreted as a criticism of the President's skill in accurately expressing his thoughts, a criticism which it is not my purpose to make.

Mr. Wilson's draft also contained a system of mandates over territories in a form which was, to say the least, rudimentary if not inadequate. By the proposed system the League of Nations, as "the residuary trustee," was to take sovereignty over "the peoples and territories" of the defeated Empires and to issue a mandate to some power or powers to exercise such sovereignty. A "residuary trustee" was a novelty in international relations sufficient to arouse conjecture as to its meaning, but giving to the League the character of an independent state with the capacity of possessing sovereignty and the power to exercise sovereign rights through a designated agent was even more extraordinary. This departure from the long accepted idea of the essentials of statehood seemed to me an inexpedient and to a degree a dangerous adventure. The only plausible excuse for the proposal seemed to be a lack of knowledge as to the nature of sovereignty and as to the attributes inherent in the very conception of a state. The character of a mandate, a mandatory, and the authority issuing the mandate presented many legal perplexities which certainly required very careful study before the experiment was tried. Until the system was fully worked out and the problems of practical operation were solved, it seemed to me unwise to suggest it and still more unwise to adopt it. While the general idea of mandates issuing from the proposed international organization was presumably acceptable to the President from the first, his support was doubtless confirmed by the fact that it followed the groove which had been made in his mind by the Smuts phrase "the heir of the Empires."

In any event it seemed to me the course of wise statesmanship to postpone the advocacy of mandates, based on the assumption that the League of Nations could become the possessor of sovereignty, until the practical application of the theory could be thoroughly considered from the standpoint of international law as well as from the standpoint of policy. The experiment was too revolutionary to be tried without hesitation and without consideration of the effect on established principles and usage. At an appropriate place this subject will be more fully discussed.

As to the organization and functions of the League of Nations planned by Mr. Wilson there was little that appealed to one who was opposed to the employment of force in compelling the observance of international obligations and to the establishment of an international oligarchy of the Great Powers to direct and control world affairs. The basic principle of the plan was that the strong should, as a matter of right recognized by treaty, possess a dominant voice in international councils. Obviously the principle of the equality of nations was ignored or abandoned. In the face of the repeated declarations of the Government of the United States in favor of the equality of independent states as to their rights in times of peace, this appeared to be a reversal of policy which it would be difficult, if not impossible, to explain in a satisfactory way. Personally I could not subscribe to this principle which was so destructive of the American theory of the proper relations between nations.

It was manifest, when I read the President's plan, that there was no possible way to harmonize my ideas with it. They were fundamentally different. There was no common basis on which to build. To attempt to bring the two theories into accord would have been futile. I, therefore, told Colonel House that it was useless to try to bring into accord the two plans, since they were founded on contradictory principles and that the only course of procedure open to me was to present my views to the President in written form, hoping that he would give them consideration, although fearing that his mind was made up, since he had ordered his plan to be printed.

In the afternoon of the same day (January 7), on which I informed the Colonel of the impossibility of harmonizing and uniting the two plans, President Wilson held a conference with the American Commissioners during which he declared that he considered the affirmative guaranty absolutely necessary to the preservation of future peace and the only effective means of preventing war. Before this declaration could be discussed M. Clemenceau was announced and the conference came to an end. While the President did not refer in any way to the "self-denying covenant" which I had proposed as a substitute, it seemed to me that he intended it to be understood that the substitute was rejected, and that he had made the declaration with that end in view. This was the nearest approach to an answer to my letter of December 23 that I ever received. Indirect as it was the implication was obvious.

Although the settled purpose of the President to insist on his form of mutual guaranty was discouraging and his declaration seemed to be intended to close debate on the subject, I felt that no effort should be spared to persuade him to change his views or at least to leave open an avenue for further consideration. Impelled by this motive I gave to the President the articles which I had drafted and asked him if he would be good enough to read them and consider the principles on which they were based. The President with his usual courtesy of manner smilingly received them. Whether or not he ever read them I cannot state positively because he never mentioned them to me or, to my knowledge, to any one else. I believe, however, that he did read them and realized that they were wholly opposed to the theory which he had evolved, because from that time forward he seemed to assume that I was hostile to his plan for a League of Nations. I drew this conclusion from the fact that he neither asked my advice as to any provision of the Covenant nor discussed the subject with me personally. In many little ways he showed that he preferred to have me direct my activities as a Commissioner into other channels and to keep away from the subject of a League. The conviction that my counsel was unwelcome to Mr. Wilson was, of course, not formed at the time that he received the articles drafted by me. It only developed after some time had elapsed, during which incidents took place that aroused a suspicion which finally became a conviction. Possibly I was over-sensitive as to the President's treatment of my communications to him. Possibly he considered my advice of no value, and, therefore, unworthy of discussion. But, in view of his letter of February 11, 1920, it must be admitted that he recognized that I was reluctant in accepting certain of his views at Paris, a recognition which arose from my declared opposition to them. Except in the case of the Shantung settlement, there was none concerning which our judgments were so at variance as they were concerning the League of Nations. I cannot believe, therefore, that I was wrong in my conclusion as to his attitude.

On the two days succeeding the one when I handed the President my draft of articles I had long conferences with Lord Robert Cecil and Colonel House. Previous to these conferences, or at least previous to the second one, I examined Lord Robert's plan for a League. His plan was based on the proposition that the Supreme War Council, consisting of the Heads of States and the Secretaries and Ministers of Foreign Affairs of the Five Great Powers, should be perpetuated as a permanent international body which should meet once a year and discuss subjects of common interest. That is, he proposed the formation of a Quintuple Alliance which would constitute itself primate over all nations and the arbiter in world affairs, a scheme of organization very similar to the one proposed by General Smuts.

Lord Robert made no attempt to disguise the purpose of his plan. It was intended to place in the hands of the Five Powers the control of international relations and the direction in large measure of the foreign policies of all nations. It was based on the power to compel obedience, on the right of the powerful to rule. Its chief merit was its honest declaration of purpose, however wrong that purpose might appear to those who denied that the possession of superior might conferred special rights upon the possessor. It seemed to provide for a rebirth of the Congress of Vienna which should be clothed in the modern garb of democracy. It could only be interpreted as a rejection of the principle of the equality of nations. Its adoption would mean that the destiny of the world would be in the hands of a powerful international oligarchy possessed of dictatorial powers.

There was nothing idealistic in the plan of Lord Robert Cecil, although he was reputed to be an idealist favoring a new international order. An examination of his plan (Appendix, page 295) shows it to be a substantial revival of the old and discredited ideas of a century ago. There could be no doubt that a plan of this sort, materialistic and selfish as it was, would win the approval and cordial support of M. Clemenceau, since it fitted in with his public advocacy of the doctrine of "the balance of power." Presumably the Italian delegates would not be opposed to a scheme which gave Italy so influential a voice in international affairs, while the Japanese, not averse to this recognition of their national power and importance, would unquestionably favor an alliance of this nature. I think that it is fair to assume that all of the Five Great Powers would have readily accepted the Cecil plan — all except the United States.

This plan, however, did not meet with the approval of President Wilson, and his open opposition to it became an obstacle which prevented its consideration in the form in which it was proposed. It is a matter of speculation what reasons appealed to the President and caused him to oppose the plan, although the principle of primacy found application in a different and less radical form in his own plan of organization. Possibly he felt that the British statesman's proposal too frankly declared the coalition and oligarchy of the Five Powers, and that there should be at least the appearance of coöperation on the part of the lesser nations. Of course, in view of the perpetual majority of the Five Powers on the Executive Council, as provided in the President's plan, the primacy of the Five was weakened little if at all by the minority membership of the small nations. The rule of unanimity gave to each nation a veto power, but no one believed that one of the lesser states represented on the Council would dare to exercise it if the Great Powers were unanimous in support of a proposition. In theory unanimity was a just and satisfactory rule; in practice it would amount to nothing. The President may also have considered the council proposed by Lord Robert to be inexpedient in view of the political organization of the United States. The American Government had no actual premier except the President, and it seemed out of the question for him to attend an annual meeting of the proposed council. It would result in the President sending a personal representative who would unavoidably be in a subordinate position when sitting with the European premiers. I think this latter reason was a very valid one, but that the first one, which seemed to appeal especially to the President, had little real merit.

In addition to his objection to the Cecil plan of administration, another was doubtless of even greater weight to Mr. Wilson and that was the entire omission in the Cecil proposal of the mutual guaranty of political independence and territorial integrity. The method of preventing wars which was proposed by Lord Robert was for the nations to enter into a covenant to submit disputes to international investigation and to obtain a report before engaging in hostilities and also a covenant not to make war on a disputant nation which accepted a report which had been unanimously adopted. He further proposed that the members of the League should undertake to regard themselves as *ipso facto* at war with a member violating these covenants and "to take, jointly and severally, appropriate military, economic, and other measures against the recalcitrant State," thus following closely the idea of the League to Enforce Peace.

Manifestly this last provision in the Cecil plan was open to the same constitutional objections as those which could be raised against the President's mutual guaranty. My impression is that Mr. Wilson's opposition to the provision was not based on the ground that it was in contravention of the Constitution of the United States, but rather on the ground that it did not go far enough in stabilizing the terms of peace which were to be negotiated. The President was seeking permanency by insuring, through the threat or pressure of international force, a condition of changelessness in boundaries and sovereign rights, subject, nevertheless, to territorial changes based either on the principle of "self-determination" or on a three-fourths vote of the Body of Delegates. He, nevertheless, discussed the subject with Lord Robert Cecil prior to laying his draft of a Covenant before the American Commissioners, as is evident by comparing it with the Cecil plan, for certain phrases are almost identical in language in the two documents.

CHAPTER VII
SELF-DETERMINATION

THE mutual guaranty which was advocated by President Wilson appears as Article III of his original draft of a Covenant. It reads as follows:

"ARTICLE III

"The Contracting Powers unite in guaranteeing to each other political independence and territorial integrity; but it is understood between them that such territorial readjustments, if any, as may in the future become necessary by reason of changes in present racial conditions and aspirations or present social and political relationships, pursuant to the principle of self-determination, and also such territorial readjustments as may in the judgment of three fourths of the Delegates be demanded by the welfare and manifest interest of the peoples concerned, may be effected if agreeable to those peoples; and that territorial changes may in equity involve material compensation. The Contracting Powers accept without reservation the principle that the peace of the world is superior in importance to every question of political jurisdiction or boundary."

In the revised draft, which he laid before the Commission on the League of Nations at its first session Article III became Article 7. It is as follows:

"ARTICLE 7

"The High Contracting Parties undertake to respect and preserve as against external aggression the territorial integrity and existing political independence of all States members of the League."

The guaranty was finally incorporated in the Treaty of Peace as Article 10. It reads:

"ARTICLE 10

"The members of the League undertake to respect and preserve as against external aggression the territorial integrity and existing political independence of all Members of the League. In case of any such aggression or in case of any threat or danger of such aggression the Council shall advise upon the means by which this obligation shall be fulfilled."

In the revision of the original draft the modifying clause providing for future territorial readjustments was omitted. It does not appear in Article 7 of the draft which was presented to the Commission on the League of Nations and which formed the basis of its deliberations. In addition to this modification the words "unite in guaranteeing" in Article III became "undertake to respect and preserve" in Article 7. These changes are only important in that they indicate a disposition to revise the article to meet the wishes, and to remove to an extent the objections, of some of the foreign delegates who had prepared plans for a League or at least had definite ideas as to the purposes and functions of an international organization.

It was generally believed that the elimination of the modifying clause from the President's original form of guaranty was chiefly due to the opposition of the states-

THE AMERICAN PEACE DELEGATION AND STAFF

men who represented the British Empire in contradis-
tinction to those who represented the self-governing
British Dominions. It was also believed that this opposition was caused by an unwillingness on their part to recognize or to apply as a right the principle of "self-determination" in arranging possible future changes of sovereignty over territories.

I do not know the arguments which were used to induce
the President to abandon this phrase and to strike it from
his article of guaranty. I personally doubt whether the
objection to the words "self-determination" was urged
upon him. Whatever reasons were advanced by his foreign colleagues, they were successful in freeing the Covenant from the phrase. It is to be regretted that the influence, which was sufficient to induce the President to eliminate from his proposed guaranty the clause containing
a formal acceptance of the principle of "self-determination," was not exerted or else was not potent enough to
obtain from him an open disavowal of the principle as a
right standard for the determination of sovereign authority. Without such a disavowal the phrase remained as
one of the general bases upon which a just peace should
be negotiated. It remained a precept of the international
creed which Mr. Wilson proclaimed while the war was
still in progress, for he had declared, in an address delivered on February 11, 1918, before a joint session of the
Senate and House of Representatives, that "self-determination is not a mere phrase. It is an imperative prin-

ciple of action which statesmen will henceforth ignore at their peril."

"Self-determination" is as right in theory as the more famous phrase "the consent of the governed," which has for three centuries been repeatedly declared to be sound by political philosophers and has been generally accepted as just by civilized peoples, but which has been for three centuries commonly ignored by statesmen because the right could not be practically applied without imperiling national safety, always the paramount consideration in international and national affairs. The two phrases mean substantially the same thing and have to an extent been used interchangeably by those who advocate the principle as a standard of right. "Self-determination" was not a new thought. It was a restatement of the old one.

Under the present political organization of the world, based as it is on the idea of nationality, the new phrase is as unsusceptible of universal application as the old one was found to be. Fixity of national boundaries and of national allegiance, and political stability would disappear if this principle was uniformly applied. Impelled by new social conditions, by economic interests, by racial prejudices, and by the various forces which affect society, change and uncertainty would result from an attempt to follow the principle in every case to which it is possible to apply it.

Among my notes I find one of December 20, 1918 — that is, one week after the American Commission landed in France — in which I recorded my thoughts concerning certain phrases or epigrams of the President, which he had declared to be bases of peace, and which I considered to contain the seeds of future trouble. In regard to the asserted right of "self-determination" I wrote:

"When the President talks of 'self-determination' what unit has he in mind? Does he mean a race, a territorial area, or a community? Without a definite unit which is practical, application of this principle is dangerous to peace and stability."

Ten days later (December 30) the frequent repetition of the phrase in the press and by members of certain groups and unofficial delegations, who were in Paris seeking to obtain hearings before the Conference, caused me to write the following:

"The more I think about the President's declaration as to the right of 'self-determination,' the more convinced I am of the danger of putting such ideas into the minds of certain races. It is bound to be the basis of impossible demands on the Peace Congress and create trouble in many lands.

"What effect will it have on the Irish, the Indians, the Egyptians, and the nationalists among the Boers? Will it not breed discontent, disorder, and rebellion? Will not the Mohammedans of Syria and Palestine and possibly of Morocco and Tripoli rely on it? How can it be harmonized with Zionism, to which the President is practically committed?

"The phrase is simply loaded with dynamite. It will raise hopes which can never be realized. It will, I fear, cost thousands of lives. In the end it is bound to be discredited, to be called the dream of an idealist who failed to realize the danger until too late to check those who attempt to put the principle in force. What a calamity that the phrase was ever uttered! What misery it will cause!"

Since the foregoing notes were written the impracticability of the universal or even of the general application of the principle has been fully demonstrated. Mr. Wilson resurrected "the consent of the governed" regardless of the fact that history denied its value as a practical guide in modern political relations. He proclaimed it in the phrase "self-determination," declaring it to be an "imperative principle of action." He made it one of the bases of peace. And yet, in the negotiations at Paris and in the formulation of the foreign policy of the United States, he has by his acts denied the existence of the right other than as the expression of a moral precept, as something to be desired, but generally unattainable in the lives of nations. In the actual conduct of affairs, in the practical and concrete relations between individuals and governments, it doubtless exercises and should exercise a measure of influence, but it is not a controlling influence.

In the Treaty of Versailles with Germany the readjustment of the German boundaries, by which the sovereignty over millions of persons of German blood was transferred to the new states of Poland and Czecho-Slovakia, and the practical cession to the Empire of Japan of the port of Kiao-Chau and control over the economic life of the Province of Shantung are striking examples of the abandonment of the principle.

In the Treaty of Saint-Germain the Austrian Tyrol was ceded to the Kingdom of Italy against the known will of substantially the entire population of that region.

In both the Treaty of Versailles and the Treaty of Saint-Germain Austria was denied the right to form a political union with Germany, and when an article of the German Constitution of August, 1919, contemplating a "reunion" of "German Austria" with the German Empire was objected to by the Supreme Council, then in session at Paris, as in contradiction of the terms of the Treaty with Germany, a protocol was signed on September 22, 1919, by plenipotentiaries of Germany and the five Principal Allied and Associated Powers, declaring the article in the Constitution null and void. There could hardly be a more open repudiation of the alleged right of "self-determination" than this refusal to permit Austria to unite with Germany however unanimous the wish of the Austrian people for such union.

But Mr. Wilson even further discredited the phrase by adopting a policy toward Russia which ignored the principle. The peoples of Esthonia, Latvia, Lithuania, the Ukraine, Georgia, and Azerbaidjan have by blood, language, and racial traits elements of difference which give to each of them in more or less degree the character of a distinct nationality. These peoples all possess aspirations to become independent states, and yet, throughout the negotiations at Paris and since that time, the Government of the United States has repeatedly refused to recognize the right of the inhabitants of these territories to determine for themselves the sovereignty under which they shall live. It has, on the contrary, declared in favor of a "Great Russia" comprising the vast territory of the old Empire except the province which belonged to the dismembered Kingdom of Poland and the lands included within the present boundaries of the Republic of Finland.

I do not mention the policy of President Wilson as to an undivided Russia by way of criticism because I believe the policy was and has continued to be the right one. The reference to it is made for the sole purpose of pointing out another example of Mr. Wilson's frequent departure without explanation from his declared standard for the determination of political authority and allegiance. I think that it must be conceded that he has by his acts proved that "self-determination" *is* "a mere phrase" which ought to be discarded as misleading because it cannot be practically applied.

It may be pointed out as a matter of special interest to the student of American history that, if the right of "self-determination" were sound in principle and uniformly applicable in establishing political allegiance and territorial sovereignty, the endeavor of the Southern States to secede from the American Union in 1861 would have been wholly justifiable; and, conversely, the Northern States, in forcibly preventing secession and compelling the inhabitants of the States composing the Confederacy to remain under the authority of the Federal Government, would have perpetrated a great and indefensible wrong against the people of the South by depriving them of a right to which they were by nature entitled. This is the logic of the application of the principle of "self-determination" to the political rights at issue in the American Civil War.

I do not believe that there are many Americans of the present generation who would support the proposition that the South was inherently right and the North was inherently wrong in that great conflict. There were, at the time when the sections were arrayed in arms against each other, and there may still be, differences of opinion as to the *legal* right of secession under the Constitution of the United States, but the inherent right of a people of a State to throw off at will their allegiance to the Federal Union and resume complete sovereignty over the territory of the State was never urged as a conclusive argument. It was the legal right and not the natural right which was emphasized as justifying those who took up arms in order to disrupt the Union. But if an American citizen denies that the principle of "self-determination" can be rightfully applied to the affairs of his own country, how can he consistently maintain that it is a right inseparable from a true conception of political liberty and therefore universally applicable, just in principle, and wise from the practical point of view?

Of course, those who subscribe to "self-determination"

and advocate it as a great truth fundamental to every political society organized to protect and promote civil liberty, do not claim it for races, peoples, or communities whose state of barbarism or ignorance deprive them of the capacity to choose intelligently their political affiliations. As to peoples or communities, however, who do possess the intelligence to make a rational choice of political allegiance, no exception is made, so far as words go, to the undeviating application of the principle. It is the affirmation of an unqualified right. It is one of those declarations of principle which sounds true, which in the abstract may be true, and which appeals strongly to man's innate sense of moral right and to his conception of natural justice, but which, when the attempt is made to apply it in every case, becomes a source of political instability and domestic disorder and not infrequently a cause of rebellion.

In the settlement of territorial rights and of the sovereignty to be exercised over particular regions there are several factors which require consideration. International boundaries may be drawn along ethnic, economic, geographic, historic, or strategic lines. One or all of these elements may influence the decision, but whatever argument may be urged in favor of any one of these factors, the chief object in the determination of the sovereignty to be exercised within a certain territory is national safety. National safety is as dominant in the life of a nation as self-preservation is in the life of an individual. It is even more so, as nations do not respond to the impulse of self-sacrifice. With national safety as the primary object to be attained in territorial settlements, the factors of the problem assume generally, though not always, the following order of importance: the strategic, to which is closely allied the geographic and historic; the economic, affecting the commercial and industrial life of a nation; and lastly the ethnic, including in the terms such conditions as consanguinity, common language, and similar social and religious institutions.

The national safety and the economic welfare of the United States were at stake in the War of Secession, although the attempt to secede resulted from institutional rather than ethnic causes. The same was true when in the Papineau Rebellion of 1837 the French inhabitants of the Province of Lower Canada attempted for ethnic reasons to free themselves from British sovereignty. Had the right of "self-determination" in the latter case been recognized as "imperative" by Great Britain, the national life and economic growth of Canada would have been strangled because the lines of communication and the commercial routes to the Atlantic seaboard would have been across an alien state. The future of Canada, with its vast undeveloped resources, its very life as a British colony, depended upon denying the right of "self-determination." It was denied and the French inhabitants of Quebec were forced against their will to accept British sovereignty.

Experience has already demonstrated the unwisdom of having given currency to the phrase "self-determination." As the expression of an actual right, the application of which is universal and invariable, the phrase has been repudiated or at least violated by many of the terms of the treaties which brought to an end the World War. Since the time that the principle was proclaimed, it has been the excuse for turbulent political elements in various lands to resist established governmental authority; it has induced the use of force in an endeavor to wrest the sovereignty over a territory or over a community from those who have long possessed and justly exercised it. It has formed the basis for territorial claims by avaricious nations. And it has introduced into domestic as well as international affairs a new spirit of disorder. It is an evil thing to permit the principle of "self-determination" to continue to have the apparent sanction of the nations when it has been in fact thoroughly discredited and will always be cast aside whenever it comes in conflict with national safety, with historic political rights, or with national economic interests affecting the prosperity of a nation.

This discussion of the right of "self-determination," which was one of the bases of peace which President Wilson declared in the winter of 1918, and which was included in the modifying clause of his guaranty as originally drafted, is introduced for the purpose of showing the reluctance which I felt in accepting his guidance in the adoption of a principle so menacing to peace and so impossible of practical application. As a matter of fact I never discussed the subject with Mr. Wilson as I purposed doing, because a situation arose on January 10, 1919, which discouraged me from volunteering to him advice on matters which did not directly pertain to legal questions and to the international administration of legal justice.

CHAPTER VIII

THE CONFERENCE OF JANUARY 10, 1919

It is with extreme reluctance, as the reader will understand, that I make any reference to the conference which the President held with the American Commissioners at the Hôtel Crillon on January 10, because of the personal nature of what occurred. It would be far more agreeable to omit an account of this unpleasant episode. But without referring to it I cannot satisfactorily explain the sudden decision I then reached to take no further part in the preparation or revision of the text of the Covenant of the League of Nations. Without explanation my subsequent conduct would be, and not without reason, open to the charge of neglect of duty and possibly of disloyalty. I do not feel called upon to rest under that suspicion, or to remain silent when a brief statement of what occurred at that conference will disclose the reason for the cessation of my efforts to effect changes in the plan of world organization which the President had prepared. In the circumstances there can be no impropriety in disclosing the truth as to the cause for a course of action when the course of action itself must be set forth to complete the record and to explain an ignorance of the subsequent negotiations regarding the League of Nations, an ignorance which has been the subject of public comment. Certainly no one who participated in the conference can object to the truth being known unless for personal reasons he prefers that a false impression should go forth. After careful consideration I can see no public reason for withholding the facts.

At this meeting, to which I refer, the President took up the provisions of his original draft of a Covenant, which was at the time in typewritten form, and indicated the features which he considered fundamental to the proper organization of a League of Nations. I pointed out certain provisions which appeared to me objectionable in principle or at least of doubtful policy. Mr. Wilson, however, clearly indicated — at least so I interpreted his words and manner — that he was not disposed to receive these criticisms in good part and was unwilling to discuss them. He also said with great candor and emphasis that he did not intend to have lawyers drafting the treaty of peace. Although this declaration was called forth by the statement that the legal advisers of the American Commission had been, at my request, preparing an outline of a treaty, a "skeleton treaty" in fact, the President's sweeping disapproval of members of the legal profession participating in the treaty-making seemed to be, and I believe was, intended to be notice to me that my counsel was unwelcome. Being the only lawyer on the delegation I naturally took this remark to myself, and I know that other American Commissioners held the same view of its purpose. If my belief was unjustified, I can only regret that I did not persevere in my criticisms and suggestions, but I could not do so believing as I then did that a lawyer's advice on any question not wholly legal in nature was unacceptable to the President, a belief which, up to the present time, I have had no reason to change.

It should be understood that this account of the conference of January 10 is given by way of explanation of my conduct subsequent to it and not in any spirit of complaint or condemnation of Mr. Wilson's attitude. He had a right to his own opinion of the worth of a lawyer's advice and a right to act in accordance with that opinion. If there was any injustice done, it was in his asking a lawyer to become a Peace Commissioner, thereby giving the impression that he desired his counsel and advice as to the negotiations in general, when in fact he did not. But, disregarding the personal element, I consider that he was justified in his course, as the entire constitutional responsibility for the negotiation of a treaty was on his shoulders and he was, in the performance of his duty, entitled to seek advice from those only in whose judgment he had confidence.

In spite of this frank avowal of prejudice by the President there was no outward change in the personal and official relations between him and myself. The breach, however, regardless of appearances, was too wide and too deep to be healed. While subsequent events bridged it temporarily, it remained until my association with President Wilson came to an end in February, 1920. I never forgot his words and always felt that in his mind my opinions, even when he sought them, were tainted with legalism.

CHAPTER IX

A RESOLUTION INSTEAD OF THE COVENANT

As it seemed advisable, in view of the incident of January 10, to have nothing to do with the drafting of the Covenant unless the entire theory was changed, the fact that there prevailed at that time a general belief that a preliminary treaty of peace would be negotiated in the near future invited an effort to delay the consideration of a complete and detailed charter of the League of Nations until the definitive treaty or a separate treaty dealing with the League alone was considered. As delay would furnish time to study and discuss the subject and prevent hasty acceptance of an undesirable or defective plan, it seemed to me that the advisable course to take was to limit reference to the organization in the preliminary treaty to general principles.

The method that I had in mind in carrying out this policy was to secure the adoption, by the Conference on the Preliminaries of Peace, of a resolution embodying a series of declarations as to the creation, the nature, and the purposes of a League of Nations, which declarations could be included in the preliminary treaty of peace accompanied by an article providing for the negotiation of a detailed plan based on these declarations at the time of the negotiation of the definitive treaty or else by an article providing for the summoning of a world congress, in which all nations, neutrals as well as belligerents, would be represented and have a voice in the drafting of a convention establishing a League of Nations in accordance with the general principles declared in the preliminary treaty. Personally I preferred a separate treaty, but doubted the possibility of obtaining the assent of the Conference to that plan because some of the delegates showed a feeling of resentment toward certain neutral nations on account of their attitude during the war, while the inclusion of the four powers which had formed the Central Alliance seemed almost out of the question.

In addition to the advantage to be gained by postponing the determination of the details of the organization until the theory, the form, the purposes and the powers of the proposed League could be thoroughly considered, it would make possible the speedy restoration of a state of peace. There can be no doubt that peace at the earliest possible moment was the supreme need of the world. The political and social chaos in the Central Empires, due to the overthrow of their strong autocratic governments and the prevailing want, suffering, and despair, in which the war had left their peoples, offered a fertile field for the pernicious doctrines of Bolshevism to take root and thrive. A proletarian revolution seemed imminent. The Spartacists in Germany, the Radical Socialists in Austria, and the Communists in Hungary were the best organized and most vigorous of the political groups in those countries and were conducting an active and seemingly successful propaganda among the starving and hopeless masses, while the Russian duumvirs, Lenine and Trotsky, were with funds and emissaries aiding these movements against established authority and social order. Eastern Europe seemed to be a volcano on the very point of eruption. Unless something was speedily done to check the peril, it threatened to spread to other countries and even to engulf the very foundations of modern civilization.

A restoration of commercial relations and of normal industrial conditions through the medium of a treaty of peace appeared to offer the only practical means of resisting these movements and of saving Europe from the horrors of a proletarian despotism which had brought the Russian people to so low a state. This was the common judgment of those who at that time watched with increasing impatience the slow progress of the negotiations at Paris and with apprehension the political turmoil in the defeated and distracted empires of Central Europe.

An immediate restoration of peace was, as I then saw it, of vital importance to the world as it was the universal demand of all mankind. To delay it for the purpose of completing the organization of a League of Nations or for any other purpose than the formulation of terms essential to peace seemed to me to be taking a risk as to the future wholly unwarranted by the relative importance of the subjects. There is no question, in the light of subsequent events, that the peoples of the Central Empires possessed a greater power of resistance to the temptations of lawlessness and disorder than was presumed in the winter of 1918–19. And yet it was a critical time. Anything might have happened. It would have taken very little to turn the scale. What occurred later cannot excuse the delay in making peace. It was not wise statesmanship and foresight that saved the world from a great catastrophe but the fortunate circumstance that a people habituated to obedience were not led astray by the enemies of the existing order.

Of the importance of negotiating a peace without waiting to complete a detailed plan for a League of Nations I was firmly convinced in those early days at Paris, and I know that the President's judgment as to this was contrary to mine. He considered — at least his course can only be so interpreted — that the organization of a League in all its details was the principal task to be accomplished by the Conference, a task that he felt must be completed before other matters were settled. The conclusion is that the necessity of an immediate peace seemed to him subordinate to the necessity of erecting an international agency to preserve the peace when it was restored. In fact one may infer that the President was disposed to employ the general longing for peace as a means of exerting pressure on the delegates in Paris and on their Governments to accept his plan for a League. It is generally believed that objections to certain provisions of the Covenant were not advanced or, if advanced, were not urged because the discussion of objections would mean delay in negotiating the peace.

Mr. Wilson gave most of his time and thought prior to his departure for the United States in February, 1919, to the revision of the plan of organization which he had prepared and to the conversion of the more influential members of the Conference to its support. While other questions vital to a preliminary peace treaty were brought up in the Council of Ten, he showed a disposition to keep them open and to avoid their settlement until the Covenant had been reported to the Conference. In this I could not conscientiously follow him. I felt that the policy was wholly wrong since it delayed the peace.

Though recognizing the President's views as to the relative importance of organizing a League and of restoring peace without delay, and suspecting that he purposed to use the impatience and fear of the delegates to break down objections to his plan of organization, I still hoped that the critical state of affairs in Europe might induce him to adopt another course. With that hope I began the preparation of a resolution to be laid before the Conference, which, if adopted, would appear in the preliminary treaty in the form of declarations which would constitute the bases of a future negotiation regarding a League of Nations.

At a conference on January 20 between the President and the American Commissioners, all being present except Colonel House, I asked the President if he did not think that, in view of the shortness of time before he would be compelled to return to Washington on account of the approaching adjournment of Congress, it would be well to prepare a resolution of this sort and to have it adopted in order that it might clear the way for the determination of other matters which should be included in a preliminary treaty. From the point of view of policy I advanced the argument that a series of declarations would draw the fire of the opponents and critics of the League and would give opportunity for an expression of American public opinion which would make possible the final drafting of the charter of a League in a way to win the approval of the great mass of the American people and in all probability insure approval of the Covenant by the Senate of the United States.

In reviewing what took place at this conference I realize now, as I did not then, that it was impolitic for me to have presented an argument based on the assumption that changes in the President's plan might be necessary, as he might interpret my words to be another effort to revise the theory of his plan. At the time, however, I was so entirely convinced of the expediency of this course, from the President's own point of view as well as from the point of view of those who gave first place to restoring peace, that I believed he would see the advantage to be gained and would adopt the course suggested. I found that I was mistaken. Mr. Wilson without discussing the subject said that he did not think that a resolution of that sort was either necessary or advisable.

While this definite rejection of the proposal seemed to close the door to further effort in that direction, I decided to make another attempt before abandoning the plan. The next afternoon (January 21) at a meeting of the Council of Ten, the discussion developed in a way that gave me an excuse to present the proposal informally to the Council. The advantages to be gained by adopting the suggested action apparently appealed to the members, and their general approval of it impressed the President, for he asked me in an undertone if I had prepared the resolution. I replied that I had been working upon it, but had ceased when he said to me the day before that he did not think it necessary or advisable, adding that I would complete the draft if he wished me to do so. He said that he would be obliged to me if I would prepare one.

Encouraged by the support received in the Council and by the seeming willingness of the President to give the proposal consideration, I proceeded at once to draft a resolution.

The task was not an easy one because it would have been useless to insert in the document any declaration which seemed to be contradictory of the President's theory of an affirmative guaranty or which was not sufficiently broad to be interpreted in other terms in the event that American public opinion was decidedly opposed to his theory, as I felt that it would be. It was also desirable, from my point of view, that the resolution should contain a declaration in favor of the equality of nations or one which would prevent the establishment of an oligarchy of the Great Powers, and another declaration which would give proper place to the administration of legal justice in international disputes.

The handicaps and difficulties under which I labored are manifest, and the resolution as drafted indicates them in that it does not express as clearly and unequivocally as it would otherwise do the principles which formed the bases of the articles which I handed to the President on January 7 and which have already been quoted *in extenso*.

The text of the resolution, which was completed on the 22d, reads as follows:

"*Resolved* that the Conference makes the following declaration:

"That the preservation of international peace is the standing policy of civilization and to that end a league of nations should be organized to prevent international wars;

"That it is a fundamental principle of peace that all nations are equally entitled to the undisturbed possession of their respective territories, to the full exercise of their respective sovereignties, and to the use of the high seas as the common property of all peoples; and

"That it is the duty of all nations to engage by mutual covenants —

"(1) To safeguard from invasion the sovereign rights of one another;

"(2) To submit to arbitration all justiciable disputes which fail of settlement by diplomatic arrangement;

"(3) To submit to investigation by the league of nations all non-justiciable disputes which fail of settlement by diplomatic arrangement; and

"(4) To abide by the award of an arbitral tribunal and to respect a report of the league of nations after investigation;

"That the nations should agree upon —

"(1) A plan for general reduction of armaments on land and sea;

"(2) A plan for the restriction of enforced military service and the governmental regulation and control of the manufacture and sale of munitions of war;

"(3) Full publicity of all treaties and international agreements;

"(4) The equal application to all other nations of commercial and trade regulations and restrictions imposed by any nation; and

"(5) The proper regulation and control of new states pending complete independence and sovereignty."

This draft of a resolution was discussed with the other American Commissioners, and after some changes of a more or less minor character which it seemed advisable to make because of the appointment of a Commission on the League of Nations at a plenary session of the Conference on January 25, of which Commission President Wilson and Colonel House were the American members, I sent the draft to the President on the 31st, four days before the Commission held its first meeting in Colonel House's office at the Hôtel Crillon.

As the Sixty-Fifth Congress would come to an end on March 4, and as the interpretation which had been placed on certain provisions of the Federal Constitution required the presence of the Chief Executive in Washington during the last days of a session in order that he might pass upon legislation enacted in the days immediately preceding adjournment, Mr. Wilson had determined that he could not remain in Paris after February 14. At the time that I sent him the proposed resolution there remained, therefore, but two weeks for the Commission on the League of Nations to organize, to deliberate, and to submit its report to the Conference, provided its report was made prior to the President's departure for the United States. It did not seem to me conceivable that the work of the Commission could be properly completed in so short a time if the President's Covenant became the basis of its deliberations. This opinion was shared by many others who appreciated the difficulties and intricacies of the subject and who felt that a hasty and undigested report would be unwise and endanger the whole plan of a world organization.

In view of this situation, which seemed to be a strong argument for delay in drafting the plan of international organization, I wrote a letter to the President, at the time I sent him the proposed resolution, saying that in my opinion no plan could be prepared with sufficient care to warrant its submission to the Conference on the Preliminaries of Peace before he left Paris and that unless a plan was reported he would be in the position of returning empty-handed to the United States. I urged him in the circumstances to secure the adoption of a resolution by the delegates similar in nature, if not in language, to the draft which was enclosed, thereby avoiding a state of affairs which would be very disheartening to the advocates of a League of Nations and cause general discontent among all peoples who impatiently expected evidence that the restoration of peace was not far distant.

It would be presumptuous on my part to speculate on the President's feelings when he received and read my letter and the proposed resolution. It was never answered or acknowledged, and he did not act upon the suggestion or discuss acting upon it, to my knowledge, with any of his colleagues. On the contrary, he summoned the Commission on the League of Nations to meet on February 3, eleven days before the date fixed for his departure for the United States, and laid before that body his revised draft of a Covenant which formed the groundwork for the Commission's report presented to the Conference on February 14.

The question naturally arises — Why did the President ask me to complete and send to him the resolution embodying a series of declarations if he did not intend to make it a subject of consideration and discussion? It is a pertinent question, but the true answer remains with Mr. Wilson himself. Possibly he concluded that the only way to obtain his plan for a League was to insist upon its practical acceptance before peace was negotiated, and that, unless he took advantage of the universal demand for peace by making the acceptance of the Covenant a condition precedent, he would be unable to obtain its adoption. While I believe this is a correct supposition, it is not responsive to the question as to the reason why he wished me to deliver to him a draft resolution. In fact it suggests another question — What, from the President's point of view, was to be gained by having the resolution in his hands?

I think the answer is not difficult to find when one remembers that Mr. Wilson had disapproved a resolution of that sort and that the Council of Ten had seemed disposed to approve it. There was no surer way to prevent me from bringing the subject again before the Council than by having the proposed resolution before him for action. Having submitted it to him I was bound, on account of our official relationship, to await his decision before taking any further steps. In a word, his request for a draft practically closed my mouth and tied my hands. If he sought to check my activities with the members of the Council in favor of the proposed course of action, he could have taken no more effectual way than the one which he did take. It was undoubtedly an effective means of "pigeonholing" a resolution, the further discussion of which might interfere with his plan to force through a report upon the Covenant before the middle of February.

This opinion as to the motive which impelled the President to pursue the course that he did in regard to a resolution was not the one held by me at the time. It was formed only after subsequent events threw new light on the subject. The delay perplexed me at the time, but the reason for it was not evident. I continued to hope, even after the Commission on the League of Nations had assembled and had begun its deliberations, that the policy of a resolution would be adopted. But, as the days went by and the President made no mention of the proposal, I realized that he did not intend to discuss it, and the conviction was forced upon me that he had never intended to have it discussed. It was a disappointing result and one which impressed me with the belief that Mr. Wilson was prejudiced against any suggestion that I might make, if it in any way differed with his own ideas even though it found favor with others.

CHAPTER X

THE GUARANTY IN THE REVISED COVENANT

DURING the three weeks preceding the meeting of the Commission on the League the work of revising the President's original draft of the Covenant had been in progress, the President and Colonel House holding frequent interviews with the more influential delegates, particularly the British and French statesmen who had been charged with the duty of studying the subject. While I cannot speak from personal knowledge, I learned that the suggested changes in terms and language were put into form by members of the Colonel's office staff. In addition to modifications which were made to meet the wishes of the foreign statesmen, especially the British, Mr. Gordon Auchincloss, the son-in-law and secretary of Colonel House, and Mr. David Hunter Miller, Auchincloss's law partner and one of the accredited legal advisers of the American Commission, prepared an elaborate memorandum on the President's draft of a Covenant which contained comments and also suggested changes in the text. On account of the intimate relations existing between Messrs. Miller and Auchincloss and Colonel House it seems reasonable to assume that their comments and suggestions were approved by, if they did not to an extent originate with, the Colonel. The memorandum was first made public by Mr. William

C. Bullitt during his hearing before the Senate Committee on Foreign Relations in September, 1919 (Senate Doc. 106, 66th Congress, 1st Session, pages 1177 *et seq.*).

The most important amendment to the Covenant suggested by these advisers was, in my judgment, the one relating to Article III of the draft, which became Article 10 in the Treaty. After a long criticism of the President's proposed guaranty, in which it is declared that "such an agreement would destroy the Monroe Doctrine," and that "any guaranty of independence and integrity means war by the guarantor if a breach of the independence or integrity of the guaranteed State is attempted and persisted in," the memorandum proposed that the following be substituted:

"Each Contracting Power severally covenants and guarantees that it will not violate the territorial integrity or impair the political independence of any other Contracting Power."

This proposed substitute should be compared with the language of the "self-denying covenant" that I sent to the President on December 23, 1918, the pertinent portion of which is repeated here for the purpose of such comparison:

"Each power signatory or adherent hereto severally covenants and guarantees that it will not violate the territorial integrity or impair the political sovereignty of any other power signatory or adherent to this convention, . . ."

The practical adoption of the language of my proposed substitute in the memorandum furnishes conclusive proof that Colonel House was "entirely converted" to my form of a guaranty as he had frankly assured me that he was on the evening of January 6. I am convinced also that Mr. Henry White and General Bliss held the same views on the subject. It is obvious that President Wilson was the only one of the American representatives at Paris who favored the affirmative guaranty, but, as he possessed the constitutional authority to determine independently the policy of the United States, his form of a guaranty was written into the revised draft of a Covenant submitted to the Commission on the League of Nations and with comparatively little change was finally adopted in the Treaty of Peace with Germany.

The memorandum prepared by Messrs. Miller and Auchincloss was apparently in the President's hands before the revised draft was completed, for certain changes in the original draft were in accord with the suggestions made in their memorandum. His failure to modify the guaranty may be considered another rejection of the "self-denying covenant" and a final decision to insist on the affirmative form of guaranty in spite of the unanimous opposition of his American colleagues.

In view of what later occurred a very definite conclusion may be reached concerning the President's rejection of the proposed substitute for his guaranty. Article 10 was from the first the storm center of opposition to the report of the Commission on the League of Nations and the chief cause for refusal of consent to the ratification of the Treaty of

Versailles by the Senate of the United States. The vulnerable nature of the provision, which had been so plainly pointed out to the President before the Covenant was submitted to the Commission, invited attack. If he had listened to the advice of his colleagues, in fact if he had listened to any American who expressed an opinion on the subject, the Treaty would probably have obtained the speedy approval of the Senate. There would have been opposition from those inimical to the United States entering any international organization, but it would have been insufficient to prevent ratification of the Treaty.

As it was, the President's unalterable determination to have his form of guaranty in the Covenant, in which he was successful, and his firm refusal to modify it in any substantial way resulted in strengthening the opponents to the League to such an extent that they were able to prevent the Treaty from obtaining the necessary consent of two thirds of the Senators.

The sincerity of Mr. Wilson's belief in the absolute necessity of the guaranty, which he proposed, to the preservation of international peace cannot be doubted. While his advisers were practically unanimous in the opinion that policy, as well as principle, demanded a change in the guaranty, he clung tenaciously to the affirmative form. The result was that which was feared and predicted by his colleagues. The President, and the President alone, must bear the responsibility for the result.

CHAPTER XI

INTERNATIONAL ARBITRATION

On the day that the Commission on the League of Nations held its first meeting and before I had reason to suspect that Mr. Wilson intended to ignore the letter which I had sent him with the suggested resolution enclosed, I determined to appeal to him in behalf of international arbitration. I decided to do this on the assumption that, even if the plan for a resolution was approved, the Commission would continue its sessions in preparation for the subsequent negotiation of an agreement of some sort providing for world organization. The provision as to arbitration in the President's original draft of a Covenant was so wrong from my point of view and showed such a lack of knowledge of the practical side of the subject that I was impelled to make an effort to induce him to change the provision. Except for the fact that the matter was wholly legal in character and invited an opinion based on technical knowledge, I would have remained silent in accordance with my feeling that it would be inadvisable for me to have anything to do with drafting the Covenant. I felt, however, that the constitution and procedure of international courts were subjects which did not affect the general theory of organization and concerning which my views might influence the President and be of aid to him in the formulation of the judicial feature of any plan adopted.

With this object in view I wrote to him the following letter:

"*Hôtel Crillon, Paris*
"*February* 3, 1919

"My dear Mr. President:

"I am deeply interested, as you know, in the constitution and procedure of international courts of arbitration, and having participated in five proceedings of this sort I feel that I can speak with a measure of authority.

"In the first place let me say that a tribunal, on which representatives of the litigants sit as judges, has not proved satisfactory even though the majority of the tribunal are nationals of other countries. However well prepared from experience on the bench to render strict justice, the litigants' arbitrators act in fact as advocates. As a consequence the neutral arbitrators are decidedly hampered in giving full and free expression to their views, and there is not that frank exchange of opinion which should characterize the conference of judges. It has generally resulted in a compromise, in which the nation in the wrong gains a measure of benefit and the nation in the right is deprived of a part of the remedy to which it is entitled. In fact an arbitration award is more of a political and diplomatic arrangement than it is a judicial determination. I believe that this undesirable result can be in large measure avoided by eliminating arbitrators of the litigant nations. It is only in the case of monetary claims that these observations do not apply.

"Another difficulty has been the method of procedure before international tribunals. This does not apply to monetary claims, but to disputes arising out of boundaries, interpretation of treaties, national rights, etc. The present method of an exchange of cases and of counter-cases is more diplomatic than judicial, since it does not put the parties in the relation of complainant and defendant. This relation can in every case be established, if not by mutual agreement, then by some agency of the League of Nations charged with that duty. Until this reform of procedure takes place there will be no definition of issues, and arbitration will continue to be the long and elaborate proceeding it has been in the past.

"There is another practical obstacle to international arbitration as now conducted which ought to be considered, and that is the cost. This obstacle does not affect wealthy nations, but it does prevent small and poor nations from resorting to it as a means of settling disputes. Just how this can be remedied I am not prepared to say, although possibly the international support of all arbitral tribunals might be provided. At any rate, I feel that something should be done to relieve the great expense which now prevents many of the smaller nations from resorting to arbitration.

"I would suggest, therefore, that the Peace Treaty contain a provision directing the League of Nations to hold a conference or to summon a conference to take up this whole matter and draft an international treaty dealing with the constitution of arbitral tribunals and radically revising the procedure.

"On account of the difficulties of the subject, which do not appear on the surface, but which experience has shown to be very real, I feel that it would be impracticable to provide in the Peace Treaty too definitely the method of constituting arbitral tribunals. It will require considerable thought and discussion to make arbitration available to the poor as well as the rich, to make an award a judicial settlement rather than a diplomatic compromise, and to supersede the cumbersome and prolonged procedure with its duplication of documents and maps by a simple method which will settle the issues and materially shorten the proceedings which now unavoidably drag along for months, if not for years.

"Faithfully yours
"ROBERT LANSING

"THE PRESIDENT
   "28 *Rue de Monceau*"

At the time that I sent this letter to Mr. Wilson I had not seen the revised draft of the Covenant which he laid before the Commission on the League of Nations. The probability is that, if I had seen it, the letter would not have been written, for in the revision of the original draft the objectionable Article V, relating to arbitration and appeals from arbitral awards, was omitted. In place of it there were substituted two articles, 11 and 12, the first being an agreement to arbitrate under certain conditions and the other providing that "the Executive Council will formulate plans for the establishment of a Permanent Court of International Justice, and this Court will be competent to hear and determine any matter which the parties recognize as suitable for submission to it for arbitration."

Unadvised as to this change, which promised a careful consideration of the method of applying legal principles of justice to international disputes, I did not feel that I could let pass without challenge the unsatisfactory provisions of the President's original draft. Knowing the

contempt which Mr. Wilson felt for The Hague Tribunal
and his general suspicion of the justice of decisions which
it might render, it seemed to me inexpedient to suggest
that it should form the basis of a newly constituted judiciary, a suggestion which I should have made had I been
dealing with any one other than President Wilson. In view
of the intensity of the President's prejudices and of the
uselessness of attempting to remove them, my letter was
intended to induce him to postpone a determination of
the subject until the problems which it presented could
be thoroughly studied and a judicial system developed by
an international body of representatives more expert in
juridical matters than the Commission on the League of
Nations, the American members of which were incom-
petent by training, knowledge, and practical experience
to consider the subject.

No acknowledgment, either written or oral, was ever
made of my letter of February 3. Possibly President Wilson considered it unnecessary to do so in view of the provision in his revised Covenant postponing discussion of the
subject. At the time, however, I naturally assumed that
my voluntary advice was unwelcome to him. His silence
as to my communications, which seemed to be intended
to discourage a continuance of them, gave the impression
that he considered an uninvited opinion on any subject
connected with the League of Nations an unwarranted interference with a phase of the negotiations which he looked
upon as his own special province, and that comment or

suggestion, which did not conform wholly to his views, was interpreted into opposition and possibly into criticism of him personally.

This judgment of the President's mental attitude, which was formed at the time, may have been too harsh. It is possible that the shortness of time in which to complete the drafting of the report of the Commission on the League of Nations, upon which he had set his heart, caused him to be impatient of any criticism or suggestion which tended to interrupt his work or that of the Commission. It may have been that pressure for time prevented him from answering letters of the character of the one of February 3. Whatever the real reason was, the fact remains that the letter went unnoticed and the impression was made that it was futile to attempt to divert the President from the single purpose which he had in mind. His fidelity to his own convictions and his unswerving determination to attain what he sought are characteristics of Mr. Wilson which are sources of weakness as well as of strength. Through them success has generally crowned his efforts, success which in some instances has been more disastrous than failure would have been.

By what means the change of Article V of the original draft of the Covenant took place, I cannot say. In the memorandum of Messrs. Miller and Auchincloss no suggestion of a Court of International Justice appears, which seems to indicate that the provision in the revised draft did not originate with them or with Colonel House. In

fact on more than one occasion I had mentioned arbitration to the Colonel and found his views on the subject extremely vague, though I concluded that he had almost as
poor an opinion of The Hague Tribunal as did the President. The probability is that the change was suggested to
Mr. Wilson by one of the foreign statesmen in a personal
interview during January and that upon sounding others
he found that they were practically unanimous in favor of
a Permanent Court of Justice. As a matter of policy it
seemed wise to forestall amendment by providing for its
future establishment. If this is the true explanation,
Article 12 was not of American origin, though it appears
in the President's revised draft.

To be entirely frank in stating my views in regard to
Mr. Wilson's attitude toward international arbitration
and its importance in a plan of world organization, I have
always been and still am skeptical of the sincerity of the
apparent willingness of the President to accept the change
which was inserted in his revised draft. It is difficult to
avoid the belief that Article V of the original draft indicated his true opinion of the application of legal principles
to controversies between nations. That article, by depriving an arbitral award of finality and conferring the
power of review on a political body with authority to
order a rehearing, shows that the President believed that
more complete justice would be rendered if the precepts
and rules of international law were in a measure subordinated to political expediency and if the judges were not

permitted to view the questions solely from the stand-point of legal justice. There is nothing that occurred, to my knowledge, between the printing of the original draft of the Covenant and the printing of the revised draft, which indicated a change of opinion by the President. It may be that this is a misinterpretation of Mr. Wilson's attitude, and that the change toward international arbitration was due to conviction rather than to expediency; but my belief is that expediency was the sole cause.

CHAPTER XII

REPORT OF COMMISSION ON LEAGUE OF NATIONS

THE Commission on the League of Nations, over which President Wilson presided, held ten meetings between February 3 and February 14, on which latter day it submitted a report at a plenary session of the Conference on the Preliminaries of Peace. The report was presented by the President in an address of exceptional excellence which made a deep impression on his hearers. His dignity of manner, his earnestness, and his logical presentation of the subject, clothed as it was in well-chosen phrases, unquestionably won the admiration of all, even of those who could not reconcile their personal views with the Covenant as reported by the Commission. It was a masterly effort, an example of literary rather than emotional oratory, peculiarly fitting to the occasion and to the temper and intellectual character of the audience.

Considering the brief time given to its discussion in the Commission and the necessary haste required to complete the document before the President's departure, the Covenant as reported to the Conference was a creditable piece of work. Many of the more glaring errors of expression and some of the especially objectionable features of the President's revised draft were eliminated. There were

A MEETING AT THE QUAI D'ORSAY AFTER PRESIDENT WILSON'S
DEPARTURE FROM PARIS

others which persisted, but the improvement was so marked that the gross defects in word and phrase largely disappeared. If one accepted the President's theory of organization, there was little to criticize in the report, except a certain inexactness of expression which indicated a lack of technical knowledge on the part of those who put the Covenant into final form. But these crudities and ambiguities of language would, it was fair to presume, disappear if the articles passed through the hands of drafting experts.

Fundamentally, however, the Covenant as reported was as wrong as the President's original draft, since it contained the affirmative guaranty of political independence and territorial integrity, the primacy of the Five Great Powers on the Executive Council, and the perplexing and seemingly unsound system of mandates. In this I could not willingly follow President Wilson, but I felt that I had done all that I could properly do in opposition to his theory. The responsibility of decision rested with him and he had made his decision. There was nothing more to be said.

On the evening of the day of the plenary session, at which the report of the League of Nations was submitted, the President left Paris for Brest where the George Washington was waiting to convey him to the United States. He carried with him the report of the Commission, whose deliberations and decisions he had so manifestly dominated. He went prepared to meet his political antagonists and the enemies of the League, confidently believing that he could win a popular support that would silence the opposition which had been increasingly manifest in the Halls of Congress and in some of the Republican newspapers which declined to follow Mr. Taft, Mr. Wickersham, Mr. Straus, and other influential Republican members of the League to Enforce Peace.

During the ten days preceding February 14, when the Commission on the League of Nations held daily sessions, the President had no conferences with the American Commissioners except, of course, with Colonel House, his American colleague on the Commission on the League. On the morning of the 14th, however, he called a meeting of the Commissioners and delivered to them the printed report which was to be presented that afternoon to the plenary session. As the meetings of the Commission on the League of Nations had been secret, the American Commissioners, other than Colonel House, were almost entirely ignorant of the proceedings and of the progress being made. Colonel House's office staff knew far more about it than did Mr. White, General Bliss, or I. When the President delivered the report to the Commissioners they were, therefore, in no position to express an opinion concerning it. The only remarks were expressions of congratulation that he had been able to complete the work before his departure. They were merely complimentary. As to the merits of the document nothing was or could be said by the three Commissioners, since no opportunity had been given them to study it, and without a critical examination any comment concerning its provisions would have been worthless. I felt and I presume that my two colleagues, who had not been consulted as to the work of the Commission on the League, felt, that it was, in any event, too late to offer suggestions or make criticisms. The report was in print; it was that afternoon to be laid before the Conference; in twelve hours the President would be on his way to the United States. Clearly it would have been useless to find fault with the report, especially if the objections related to the fundamental ideas of the organization which it was intended to create. The President having in the report declared the American policy, his commissioned representatives were bound to acquiesce in his decision whatever their personal views were. Acquiescence or resignation was the choice, and resignation would have undoubtedly caused an unfortunate, if not a critical, situation. In the circumstances acquiescence seemed the only practical and proper course.

The fact that in ten meetings and in a week and a half a Commission composed of fifteen members, ten of whom represented the Five Great Powers and five of whom represented the lesser powers (to which were later added four others), completed the drafting of a detailed plan of a League of Nations, is sufficient in itself to raise doubts as to the thoroughness with which the work was done and as to the care with which the various plans and numerous provisions proposed were studied, compared, and discussed. It gives the impression that many clauses were accepted under the pressing necessity of ending the Commission's labors within a fixed time. The document itself bears evidence of the haste with which it was prepared, and is almost conclusive proof in itself that it was adopted through personal influence rather than because of belief in the wisdom of all its provisions.

The Covenant of the League of Nations was intended to be the greatest international compact that had ever been written. It was to be the *Maxima Charta* of mankind securing to the nations their rights and liberties and uniting them for the preservation of universal peace. To harmonize the conflicting views of the members of the Commission — and it was well known that they were conflicting — and to produce in eleven days a world charter, which would contain the elements of greatness or even of perpetuity, was on the face of it an undertaking impossible of accomplishment. The document which was produced sufficiently establishes the truth of this assertion.

It required a dominant personality on the Commission to force through a detailed plan of a League in so short a time. President Wilson was such a personality. By adopting the scheme of an oligarchy of the Great Powers he silenced the dangerous opposition of the French and British members of the Commission who willingly passed over minor defects in the plan provided this Concert of Powers, this Quintuple Alliance, was incorporated in the Covenant. And for the same reason it may be assumed the Japanese and Italians found the President's plan acceptable. Mr. Wilson won a great personal triumph, but he did so by surrendering the fundamental principle of the equality of nations. In his eagerness to "make the world safe for democracy" he abandoned international democracy and became the advocate of international autocracy.

It is not my purpose to analyze the provisions of the Covenant which was submitted to the Conference on the Preliminaries of Peace on February 14, 1919. My objections to it have been sufficiently discussed in the preceding pages. It would be superfluous to repeat them. The innumerable published articles and the endless debates on the Covenant have brought out its good features as well as its defects. Unfortunately for the opponents and defenders of the document alike some of the objections urged have been flagrantly unjustifiable and based on false premises and misstatements of fact and of law, which seem to show political motives and not infrequently personal animosity toward Mr. Wilson. The exaggerated statements and unfair arguments of some of the Senators, larded, as they often were, with caustic sarcasm and vindictive personalities, did much to prevent an honest and useful discussion of the merits and demerits of the Covenant.

The effect upon President Wilson of this campaign against him personally — and it seems to me that it would have had the same effect upon any man of spirit — was to arouse his indignation. Possibly a less stubborn man would not have assumed so uncompromising an attitude as he did or have permitted his ire to find expression in threats, but it cannot be denied that there was provocation for the resentment which he exhibited. The President has been blamed for not having sought more constantly to placate the opponents of the Covenant and to meet them on a common ground of compromise, especially during his visit to the United States in February, 1919. From the point of view of policy there is justice in blaming him, but, when one considers the personal animus shown and the insolent tone assumed by some of his critics, his conduct was very human; not wise, but human. Mr. Wilson had never shown a spirit of conciliation in dealing with those who opposed him. Even in the case of a purely political question he appeared to consider opposition to be a personal affront and he was disposed to retaliate in a personal way. In a measure this explains the personal enmity of many of his political foes. I think that it is not unjust to say that President Wilson was stronger in his hatreds than in his friendships. He seemed to lack the ability to forgive one who had in any way offended him or opposed him.

Believing that much of the criticism of the Covenant was in reality criticism of him as its author, a belief that was in a measure justified, the President made it a personal matter. He threatened, in a public address delivered in the New York Opera House on the eve of his departure for France, to force the Republican majority to accept the Covenant by interweaving the League of Nations into the terms of peace to such an extent that they could not be separated, so that, if they rejected the League, they would be responsible for defeating the Treaty and preventing a restoration of peace. With the general demand for peace this seemed no empty threat, although the propriety of making it may be questioned. It had, however, exactly the opposite effect from that which the President intended. Its utterance proved to be as unwise as it was ineffective. The opposition Senators resented the idea of being coerced. They became more than ever determined to defeat a President whom they charged with attempting to disregard and nullify the right of the Senate to exercise independently its constitutional share in the treaty-making power. Thus at the very outset of the struggle between the President and the Senate a feeling of hostility was engendered which continued with increasing bitterness on both sides and prevented any compromise or concession in regard to the Covenant as it finally appeared in the Treaty of Versailles.

When President Wilson returned to Paris after the adjournment of the Sixty-Fifth Congress on March 4, 1919, he left behind him opponents who were stronger and more confident than they were when he landed ten days before. While his appeal to public opinion in favor of the League of Nations had been to an extent successful, there was a general feeling that the Covenant as then drafted required amendment so that the sovereign rights and the traditional policies of the United States should be safeguarded. Until the document was amended it seemed that the opposition had the better of the argument with the people. Furthermore, when the new Congress met, the Republicans would have a majority in the Senate which was of special importance in the matter of the Treaty which would contain the Covenant, because it would, when sent to the Senate, be referred to the Committee on Foreign Relations to report on its ratification and a majority of that Committee, under a Republican organization, would presumably be hostile to the plan for a League advocated by the President. The Committee could hinder and possibly prevent the acceptance of the Covenant, while it would have the opportunity to place the opposition's case in a favorable light before the American people and to attack the President's conduct of the negotiations at Paris.

I believe that the President realized the loss of strategic position which he had sustained by the Democratic defeat at the polls in November, 1918, but was persuaded that, by making certain alterations in the Covenant suggested by Republicans favorable to the formation of a League, and especially those advocating a League to Enforce Peace, he would be able to win sufficient support in the Senate and from the people to deprive his antagonists of the advantage which they had gained by the elections. This he sought to do on his return to Paris about the middle of March. If the same spirit of compromise had been shown while he was in America it would doubtless have gone far to weaken hostility to the Covenant. Unfortunately for his purpose he assumed a contrary attitude, and in consequence the sentiment against the League was crystallized and less responsive to the concessions which the President appeared willing to make when the Commission on the League of Nations resumed its sittings, especially as the obnoxious Article 10 remained intact.

In the formulation of the amendments to the Covenant, which were incorporated in it after the President's return from the United States and before its final adoption by the Conference, I had no part and I have no reason to think that Mr. White or General Bliss shared in the work. As these amendments or modifications did not affect the theory of organization or the fundamental principles of the League, they in no way changed my views or lessened the differences between the President's judgment and mine. Our differences were as to the bases and not as to the details of the Covenant. Since there was no disposition to change the former we were no nearer an agreement than we were in January.

The President's visit to the United States had been disappointing to the friends of a League in that he had failed to rally to the support of the Covenant an overwhelming popular sentiment in its favor which the opposition in the Senate could not resist. The natural reaction was that the peoples of Europe and their statesmen lost a measure of their enthusiasm and faith in the project. Except in the case of a few idealists, there was a growing disposition to view it from the purely practical point of view and to speculate on its efficacy as an instrument to interpret and carry out the international will. Among the leaders of political thought in the principal Allied countries, the reports of the President's reception in the United States were sufficiently conflicting to arouse doubt as to whether the American people were actually behind him in his plan for a League, and this doubt was not diminished by his proposed changes in the Covenant, which indicated that he was not in full control of the situation at home.

Two weeks after the President had resumed his duties as a negotiator and had begun the work of revising the Covenant, I made a memorandum of my views as to the situation that then existed. The memorandum is as follows:

"*March* 25, 1919

"With the increasing military preparations and operations throughout Eastern Europe and the evident purpose of all these quarreling nations to ignore any idea of disarmament and to rely upon force to obtain and retain territory and rights, the League of Nations is being discussed with something like contempt by the cynical, hardheaded statesmen of those countries which are being put on a war-footing. They are cautious and courteous out of regard for the President. I doubt if the truth reaches him, but it comes to me from various sources.

"These men say that in theory the idea is all right and is an ideal to work toward, but that under present conditions it is not practical in preventing war. They ask, what nation is going to rely on the guaranty in the Covenant if a jealous or hostile neighbor maintains a large army. They want to know whether it would be wise or not to disarm under such conditions. Of course the answers are obvious.

But, if the guaranty is not sufficient, or accepted as sufficient, protection, what becomes of the central purpose of the League and the chief reason for creating it?

"I believe that the President and Colonel House see this, though they do not admit it, and that to save the League from being cast into the discard they will attempt to make of it a sort of international agency to do certain things which would normally be done by independent international commissions. Such a course would save the League from being still-born and would so interweave it with the terms of peace that to eliminate it would be to open up some difficult questions.

"Of course the League of Nations as originally planned had one supreme object and that was to prevent future wars. That was substantially all that it purposed to do. Since then new functions have been gradually added until the chief argument for the League's existence has been almost lost to sight. The League has been made a convenient 'catch-all' for all sorts of international actions. At first this was undoubtedly done to give the League something to do, and now it is being done to save it from extinction or from being ignored.

"I am not denying that a common international agent may be a good thing. In fact the plan has decided merit. But the organization of the League does not seem to me suitable to perform efficiently and properly these new functions.

"However, giving this character to the League may save it from being merely an agreeable dream. As the repository of international controversies requiring long and careful consideration it may live and be useful.

"My impression is that the principal sponsors for the League are searching through the numerous disputes which are clogging the wheels of the Conference, seizing upon every one which can possibly be referred, and heaping them on the League of Nations to give it standing as a useful and necessary adjunct to the Treaty.

"At least that is an interesting view of what is taking place and opens a wide field for speculation as to the future of the League and the verdict which history will render as to its origin, its nature, and its real value."

I quote this memorandum because it gives my thoughts at the time concerning the process of weaving the League into the terms of peace as the President had threatened to do. I thought then that it had a double purpose, to give a practical reason for the existence of the League and to make certain the ratification of the Covenant by the Senate. No fact has since developed which has induced me to change my opinion.

In consequence of the functions which were added to the League, the character of the League itself underwent a change. Instead of an agency created solely for the prevention of international wars, it was converted into an agency to carry out the terms of peace. Its idealistic conception was subordinated to the materialistic purpose of confirming to the victorious nations the rewards of victory. It is true that during the long struggle between the President and the Senate on the question of ratification there was in the debates a general return to the original purpose of the League by both the proponents and opponents of the Covenant, but that fact in no way affects the truth of the assertion that, in order to save the League of Nations, its character was changed by extending its powers and duties as a common agent of the nations which had triumphed over the Central Alliance.

The day before the Treaty of Peace was delivered to the German plenipotentiaries (May 6) its terms induced me to write a note entitled "The Greatest Loss Caused by the War," referring to the loss of idealism to the world. In that note I wrote of the League of Nations as follows:

"Even the measure of idealism, with which the League of Nations was at the first impregnated, has, under the influence and intrigue of ambitious statesmen of the Old World, been supplanted by an open recognition that force and selfishness are primary elements in international co-operation. The League has succumbed to this reversion to a cynical materialism. It is no longer a creature of idealism. Its very source and reason have been dried up and have almost disappeared. The danger is that it will become a bulwark of the old order, a check upon all efforts to bring man again under the influence which he has lost."

The President, in the addresses which he afterward made in advocacy of the Covenant and of ratification of the Treaty, indicated clearly the wide divergence of opinion between us as to the character of the League provided for in the Treaty. I do not remember that the subject was directly discussed by us, but I certainly took no pains to hide my misgivings as to the place it would have in the international relations of the future. However, as Mr. Wilson knew that I disapproved of the theory and basic principles of the organization, especially the recognition of the oligarchy of the Five Powers, he could not but realize that I considered that idealism had given place to political expediency in order to secure for the Covenant the support of the powerful nations represented at the Conference. This was my belief as to our relations when the Treaty of Peace containing the Covenant was laid before the Germans at the Hôtel des Reservoirs in Versailles.

CHAPTER XIII
THE SYSTEM OF MANDATES

In the foregoing review of the opposite views held by the President and by me in regard to the plan for a League of Nations and specifically in regard to the Covenant as originally drawn and as revised, mention was made of the proposed mandatory system as one of the subjects concerning which we were not in agreement. My objections to the system were advanced chiefly on the ground of the legal difficulties which it presented because it seemed probable that the President would give more weight to my opinion on that ground than on one which concerned the policy of adopting the system. Viewed from the latter standpoint it appeared to me most unwise for the President to propose a plan, in which the United States would be expected to participate and which, if it did participate, would involve it in the political quarrels of the Old World. To do so would manifestly require a departure from the traditional American policy of keeping aloof from the political jealousies and broils of Europe. Without denying that present conditions have, of necessity, modified the old policy of isolation and without minimizing the influence of that fact on the conduct of American foreign affairs, it did not seem essential for the United States to become the guardian of any of the peoples of the Near East, who were

aspiring to become independent nationalities, a guardian-
ship which the President held to be a duty that the United
States was bound to perform as its share of the burden
imposed by the international coöperation which he considered vital to the new world order.

The question of mandates issuing from the League of
Nations was discussed at length by the Council of Ten in
connection with the disposition and future control of the
German colonies and incidentally as to the dismemberment of the Ottoman Empire. The discussions were chiefly
along the lines of practicability, of policy, and of moral
obligation. The President's strong support of the mandatory system and his equally strong objection to the idea of
condominium showed that his mind was made up in favor
of the issuance of mandates by the League. Since it would
have been highly improper for me to oppose openly a
policy which the President had declared under his constitutional authority, there was no proper opportunity to
present the legal difficulties of the system to the Council.

However, the seriousness of these difficulties and the
possible troubles and controversies which might be anticipated from attempting to put the system into operation
induced me, after one of the sessions of the Council of
Ten, to state briefly to the President some of the serious
objections to League mandates from the standpoint of international law and the philosophy of government. President Wilson listened with his usual attentiveness to what
I had to say, though the objections evidently did not appeal

to him, as he characterized them as "mere technicalities" which could be cured or disregarded. Impressed myself with the importance of these "technicalities" and their direct bearing on the policy of adopting the mandatory system, I later, on February 2, 1919, embodied them in a memorandum. At the time I hoped and believed that the negotiation of the completed Covenant might be postponed and that there would be another opportunity to raise the question. The memorandum, prepared with this end in view, is as follows:

"The system of 'mandatories under the League of Nations,' when applied to territories which were formerly colonies of Germany, the system which has been practically adopted and will be written into the plan for the League, raises some interesting and difficult questions:

"The one, which is the most prominent since it enters into nearly all of the international problems presented, is —Where does the sovereignty over these territories reside?

"Sovereignty is inherent in the very conception of government. It cannot be destroyed, though it may be absorbed by another sovereignty either by compulsion or cession. When the Germans were ousted from their colonies, the sovereignty passed to the power or powers which took possession. The location of the sovereignty up to the present is clear, but with the introduction of the League of Nations as an international primate superior to the conquerors some rather perplexing questions will have to be answered.

"Do those who have seized the sovereignty transfer it or does Germany transfer it to the League of Nations? If so, how?

"Does the League assume possession of the sovereignty on its renunciation by Germany? If so, how?

"Does the League merely direct the disposition of the sovereignty without taking possession of it?

"Assuming that the latter question is answered in the affirmative, then after such disposition of the right to exercise sovereignty, which will presumably be a limited right, where does the actual sovereignty reside?

"The appointment of a mandatory to exercise sovereign rights over territory is to create an agent for the real sovereign. But who is the real sovereign?

"Is the League of Nations the sovereign, or is it a common agent of the nations composing the League, to whom is confided solely the duty of naming the mandatory and issuing the mandate?

"If the League is the sovereign, can it avoid responsibility for the misconduct of the mandatory, its agent?

"If it is not the League, who is responsible for the mandatory's conduct?

"Assuming that the mandatory in faithfully performing the provisions of the mandate unavoidably works an injustice upon another party, can or ought the mandatory to be held responsible? If not, how can the injured party obtain redress? Manifestly the answer is, 'From the sovereign,' but who is the sovereign?

"In the Treaty of Peace Germany will be called upon to renounce sovereignty over her colonial possessions. To whom will the sovereignty pass?

"If the reply is, 'The League of Nations,' the question is: Does the League possess the attributes of an independent state so that it can function as an owner of territory? If so, what is it? A world state?

"If the League does not constitute a world state, then the sovereignty would have to pass to some national state.

What national state? What would be the relation of the national state to the League?

"If the League is to receive title to the sovereignty, what officers of the League are empowered to receive it and to transfer its exercise to a mandatory?

"What form of acceptance should be adopted?

"Would every nation which is a member of the League have to give its representatives full powers to accept the title?

"Assuming that certain members decline to issue such powers or to accept title as to one or more of the territories, what relation would those members have to the mandatory named?"

There is no attempt in the memorandum to analyze or classify the queries raised, and, as I review them in the light of the terms of the Treaty of Versailles, I do not think that some of them can be asked with any helpful purpose. On the other hand, many of the questions, I believe the large majority, were as pertinent after the Treaty was completed as they were when the memorandum was made.

As Colonel House was the other member of the Commission on the League of Nations and would have to consider the practicability and expediency of including the mandatory system in the Covenant, I read the memorandum to him stating that I had orally presented most of the questions to the President who characterized them as "legal technicalities" and for that reason unimportant. I said to the Colonel that I differed with the President, as I hoped he did, not only as to the importance of considering the difficulties raised by the questions before the system of mandates was adopted, but also as to the importance of viewing from every standpoint the wisdom of the system and the difficulties that might arise in its practical operation. I stated that, in my opinion, a simpler and better plan was to transfer the sovereignty over territory to a particular nation by a treaty of cession under such terms as seemed wise and, in the case of some of the newly erected states, to have them execute treaties accepting protectorates by Powers mutually acceptable to those states and to the League of Nations.

Colonel House, though he listened attentively to the memorandum and to my suggestions, did not seem convinced of the importance of the questions or of the advantages of adopting any other plan than that of the proposed mandatory system. To abandon the system meant to abandon one of the ideas of international supervision, which the President especially cherished and strongly advocated. It meant also to surrender one of the proposed functions of the League as an agent in carrying out the peace settlements under the Treaty, functions which would form the basis of an argument in favor of the organization of the League and furnish a practical reason for its existence. Of course the presumed arguments against the abandonment of mandates may not have been considered, but at the time I believed that they were potent with Colonel House and with the President. The subsequent advocacy of the system by these two influential members of the Commission on the League of Nations, which resulted in its adoption, in no way lessened my belief as to the reasons for their support.

The mandatory system, a product of the creative mind of General Smuts, was a novelty in international relations which appealed strongly to those who preferred to adopt unusual and untried methods rather than to accept those which had been tested by experience and found practical of operation. The self-satisfaction of inventing something new or of evolving a new theory is inherent with not a few men. They are determined to try out their ideas and are impatient of opposition which seeks to prevent the experiment. In fact opposition seems sometimes to enhance the virtue of a novelty in the minds of those who propose or advocate its adoption. Many reformers suffer from this form of vanity.

In the case of the system of mandates its adoption by the Conference and the conferring on the League of Nations the power to issue mandates seemed at least to the more conservative thinkers at Paris a very doubtful venture. It appeared to possess no peculiar advantages over the old method of transferring and exercising sovereign control either in providing added protection to the inhabitants of territory subject to a mandate or greater certainty of international equality in the matter of commerce and trade, the two principal arguments urged in favor of the proposed system.

If the advocates of the system intended to avoid through its operation the appearance of taking enemy

territory as the spoils of war, it was a subterfuge which de-
ceived no one. It seemed obvious from the very first that
the Powers, which under the old practice would have obtained sovereignty over certain conquered territories,
would not be denied mandates over those territories. The
League of Nations might reserve in the mandate a right
of supervision of administration and even of revocation
of authority, but that right would be nominal and of little,
if any, real value provided the mandatory was one of the
Great Powers as it undoubtedly would be. The almost
irresistible conclusion is that the protagonists of the theory
saw in it a means of clothing the League of Nations with
an apparent usefulness which justified the League by making it the guardian of uncivilized and semi-civilized peoples
and the international agent to watch over and prevent
any deviation from the principle of equality in the commercial and industrial development of the mandated
territories.

It may appear surprising that the Great Powers so
readily gave their support to the new method of obtaining
an apparently limited control over the conquered territories, and did not seek to obtain complete sovereignty
over them. It is not necessary to look far for a sufficient
and very practical reason. If the colonial possessions of
Germany had, under the old practice, been divided among
the victorious Powers and been ceded to them directly in
full sovereignty, Germany might justly have asked that
the value of such territorial cessions be applied on any war

indemnities to which the Powers were entitled. On the other hand, the League of Nations in the distribution of mandates would presumably do so in the interests of the inhabitants of the colonies and the mandates would be accepted by the Powers as a duty and not to obtain new possessions. Thus under the mandatory system Germany lost her territorial assets, which might have greatly reduced her financial debt to the Allies, while the latter obtained the German colonial possessions without the loss of any of their claims for indemnity. In actual operation the apparent altruism of the mandatory system worked in favor of the selfish and material interests of the Powers which accepted the mandates. And the same may be said of the dismemberment of Turkey. It should not be a matter of surprise, therefore, that the President found little opposition to the adoption of his theory, or, to be more accurate, of the Smuts theory, on the part of the European statesmen.

There was one case, however, in which the issuance of a mandate appeared to have a definite and practical value and to be superior to a direct transfer of complete sovereignty or of the conditional sovereignty resulting from the establishment of a protectorate. The case was that of a territory with or without a national government, which, not being self-supporting and not sufficiently strong to protect its borders from aggressive neighbors, or its people sufficiently enlightened to govern themselves properly, would be a constant source of expense instead of profit to the Power, which as its protector and tutor became its overlord. Under such conditions there was more probability of persuading a nation inspired by humanitarian and altruistic motives to assume the burden for the common good under the mandatory system than under the old method of cession or of protectorate. As to nations, however, which placed national interests first and made selfishness the standard of international policy it was to be assumed that an appeal under either system would be ineffective.

The truth of this was very apparent at Paris. In the tentative distribution of mandates among the Powers, which took place on the strong presumption that the mandatory system would be adopted, the principal European Powers appeared to be willing and even eager to become mandatories over territories possessing natural resources which could be profitably developed and showed an unwillingness to accept mandates for territories which, barren of mineral or agricultural wealth, would be continuing liabilities rather than assets. This is not stated by way of criticism, but only in explanation of what took place.

From the beginning to the end of the discussions on mandates and their distribution among the Powers it was repeatedly declared that the United States ought to participate in the general plan for the upbuilding of the new states which under mandatories would finally become independent nationalities, but it was never, to my knowledge, proposed, except by the inhabitants of the region in question, that the United States should accept a mandate for Syria or the Asiatic coast of the Ægean Sea. Those regions were rich in natural resources and their economic future under a stable government was bright. Expenditures in their behalf and the direction of their public affairs would bring ample returns to the mandatory nations. On the other hand, there was a sustained propaganda—for it amounted to that—in favor of the United States assuming mandates over Armenia and the municipal district of Constantinople, both of which, if limited by the boundaries which it was then purposed to draw, would be a constant financial burden to the Power accepting the mandate, and, in the case of Armenia, would require that Power to furnish a military force estimated at not less than 50,000 men to prevent the aggression of warlike neighbors and to preserve domestic order and peace.

It is not too severe to say of those who engaged in this propaganda that the purpose was to take advantage of the unselfishness of the American people and of the altruism and idealism of President Wilson in order to impose on the United States the burdensome mandates and to divide those which covered desirable territories among the European Powers. I do not think that the President realized at the time that an actual propaganda was going on, and I doubt very much whether he would have believed it if he had been told. Deeply impressed with the

idea that it was the moral duty of the great and enlightened nations to aid the less fortunate and especially to
guard the nationalities freed from autocratic rule until
they were capable of self-government and self-protection,
the President apparently looked upon the appeals made
to him as genuine expressions of humanitarianism and
as manifestations of the opinion of mankind concerning
the part that the United States ought to take in the
reconstruction of the world. His high-mindedness and
loftiness of thought blinded him to the sordidness of purpose which appears to have induced the general acquiescence in his desired system of mandates, and the same
qualities of mind caused him to listen sympathetically to
proposals, the acceptance of which would give actual proof
of the unselfishness of the United States.

Reading the situation thus and convinced of the objections against the mandatory system from the point of
view of international law, of policy and of American interests, I opposed the inclusion of the system in the plan
for a League of Nations. In view of the attitude which
Mr. Wilson had taken toward my advice regarding policies I confined the objections which I presented to him, as
I have stated, to those based on legal difficulties. The objections on the ground of policy were made to Colonel
House in the hope that through him they might reach the
President and open his eyes to the true state of affairs.
Whether they ever did reach him I do not know. Nothing
in his subsequent course of action indicated that they did.

But, if they did, he evidently considered them as invalid as he did the objections arising from legal difficulties. The system of mandates was written into the Treaty and a year after the Treaty was signed President Wilson asked the Congress for authority to accept for the United States a mandate over Armenia. This the Congress refused. It is needless to make further comment.

CHAPTER XIV

DIFFERENCES AS TO THE LEAGUE RECAPITULATED

THE differences between the President's views and mine in regard to the character of the League of Nations and to the provisions of the Covenant relating to the organization and functions of the League were irreconcilable, and we were equally in disagreement as to the duties of the League in carrying out certain provisions of the Treaty of Peace as the common agent of the signatory Powers. As a commissioned representative of the President of the United States acting under his instructions I had no alternative but to accept his decisions and to follow his directions, since surrender of my commission as Peace Commissioner seemed to me at the time to be practically out of the question. I followed his directions, however, with extreme reluctance because I felt that Mr. Wilson's policies were fundamentally wrong and would unavoidably result in loss of prestige to the United States and to him as its Chief Magistrate. It seemed to me that he had endangered, if he had not destroyed, his preëminent position in world affairs in order to obtain the acceptance of his plan for a League of Nations, a plan which in theory and in detail was so defective that it would be difficult to defend it successfully from critical attack.

The objections to the terms of the Covenant, which I

had raised at the outset, were based on principle and also on policy, as has been shown in the preceding pages; and on the same grounds I had opposed their hasty adoption and their inclusion in the Peace Treaty to be negotiated at Paris by the Conference. These objections and the arguments advanced in their support did not apparently have any effect on President Wilson, for they failed to change his views or to modify the plan which he, with General Smuts and Lord Robert Cecil, had worked out for an international organization. They did not swerve him one jot from his avowed purpose to make the creation of the League of Nations the principal feature of the negotiations and the provisions of the Covenant the most prominent articles in the Treaties of Peace with the Central Powers.

Instead of accomplishing their designed purpose, my efforts to induce the President to change his policy resulted only in my losing his confidence in my judgment and in arousing in his mind, if I do not misinterpret his conduct, doubts of my loyalty to him personally. It was characteristic of Mr. Wilson that his firm conviction as to the soundness of his conclusions regarding the character of the League of Nations and his fixity of purpose in seeking to compel its adoption by the Peace Conference were so intense as to brook no opposition, especially from one whom he expected to accept his judgment without question and to give support in thought and word to any plan or policy which he advocated. In view of this mental attitude of the President it is not difficult to understand his opinion of my course of action at Paris. The breach in our confidential relations was unavoidable in view of my conviction of the duty of an official adviser and his belief that objections ought not to be urged as to a matter concerning which he had expressed his opinion. To give implied assent to policies and intentions which seemed to me wrong or unwise would have been violative of a public trust, though doubtless by remaining silent I might have won favor and approval from the President and retained his confidence.

In summarizing briefly the subjects of disagreement between the President and myself concerning the League of Nations I will follow the order of importance rather than the order in which they arose. While they also divide into two classes, those based on principle and those based on policy, it does not seem advisable to treat them by classes in the summary.

The most serious defect in the President's Covenant was, in my opinion, one of principle. It was the practical denial of the equality of nations in the regulation of international affairs in times of peace through the recognition in the Executive Council of the League of the right of primacy of the Five Great Powers. This was an abandonment of a fundamental principle of international law and comity and was destructive of the very conception of national sovereignty both as a term of political philosophy and as a term of constitutional law. The denial of the equal independence and the free exercise of sovereign rights of all states in the conduct of their foreign affairs, and the establishment of this group of primates, amounted to a recognition of the doctrine that the powerful are, in law as well as in fact, entitled to be the overlords of the weak. If adopted, it legalized the mastery of might, which in international relations, when peace prevailed, had been universally condemned as illegal and its assertion as reprehensible.

It was this doctrine, that the possessors of superior physical power were as a matter of right the supervisors, if not the dictators, of those lacking the physical power to resist their commands, which was the vital element of ancient imperialism and of modern Prussianism. Belief in it as a true theory of world polity justified the Great War in the eyes of the German people even when they doubted the plea of their Government that their national safety was in peril. The victors, although they had fought the war with the announced purpose of proving the falsity of this pernicious doctrine and of emancipating the oppressed nationalities subject to the Central Powers, revived the doctrine with little hesitation during the negotiations at Paris and wrote it into the Covenant of the League of Nations by contriving an organization which would give practical control over the destinies of the world to an oligarchy of the Five Great Powers. It was an assumption of the right of supremacy based on the fact that the united strength of these Powers could compel obedience. It was a full endorsement of the theory of "the balance of power" in spite of the recognized evils of that doctrine in its practical application. Beneath the banner of the democracies of the world was the same sinister idea which had found expression in the Congress of Vienna with its purpose of protecting the monarchical institutions of a century ago. It proclaimed in fact that mankind must look to might rather than right, to force rather than law, in the regulation of international affairs for the future.

This defect in the theory, on which the League of Nations was to be organized, was emphasized and given permanency by the adoption of a mutual guaranty of territorial integrity and political independence against external aggression. Since the burden of enforcing the guaranty would unavoidably fall upon the more powerful nations, they could reasonably demand the control over affairs which might develop into a situation requiring a resort to the guaranty. In fact during a plenary session of the Peace Conference held on May 31, 1919, President Wilson stated as a broad principle that responsibility for protecting and maintaining a settlement under one of the Peace Treaties carried with it the right to determine what that settlement should be. The application to the case of responsible guarantors is obvious and was apparently in mind when the Covenant was being evolved. The same principle was applied throughout the negotiations at Paris.

The mutual guaranty from its affirmative nature compelled in fact, though not in form, the establishment of a ruling group, a coalition of the Great Powers, and denied, though not in terms, the equality of nations. The oligarchy was the logical result of entering into the guaranty or the guaranty was the logical result of the creation of the oligarchy through the perpetuation of the basic idea of the Supreme War Council. No distinction was made as to a state of war and a state of peace. Strongly opposed to the abandonment of the principle of the equality of nations in times of peace I naturally opposed the affirmative guaranty and endeavored to persuade the President to accept as a substitute for it a self-denying or negative covenant which amounted to a promise of "hands-off" and in no way required the formation of an international oligarchy to make it effective.

In addition to the foregoing objection I opposed the guaranty on the ground that it was politically inexpedient to attempt to bind the United States by a treaty provision which by its terms would certainly invite attack as to its constitutionality. Without entering into the strength of the legal argument, and without denying that there are two sides to the question, the fact that it was open to debate whether the treaty-making power under the Constitution could or could not obligate the Government of the United States to make war under certain conditions was in my judgment a practical reason for avoiding the issue. If the power existed to so bind the United States by treaty on the theory that the Federal Government could not be restricted in its right to make international agreements, then the guaranty would be attacked as an unwise and needless departure from the traditional policies of the Republic. If the power did not exist, then the violation of the Constitution would be an effective argument against such an undertaking. Whatever the conclusion might be, therefore, as to the legality of the guaranty or as to whether the obligation was legal or moral in nature, it did not seem possible for it to escape criticism and vigorous attack in America.

It seemed to me that the President's guaranty was so vulnerable from every angle that to insist upon it would endanger the acceptance of any treaty negotiated if the Covenant was, in accordance with the President's plan, made an integral part of it. Then, too, opposition would, in my opinion, develop on the ground that the guaranty would permit European Powers to participate, if they could not act independently, in the forcible settlement of international quarrels in the Western Hemisphere whenever there was an actual invasion of territory or violation of sovereignty, while conversely the United States would be morally, if not legally, bound to take part in coercive measures in composing European differences under similar conditions. It could be urged with much force that the Monroe Doctrine in the one case and the Washington policy of avoiding "entangling alliances" in the other would be so affected that they would both have to be substantially abandoned or else rewritten. If the American people were convinced that this would be the consequence of accepting the affirmative guaranty, it meant its rejection. In any event it was bound to produce an acrimonious controversy. From the point of view of policy alone it seemed unwise to include the guaranty in the Covenant, and believing that an objection on that ground would appeal to the President more strongly than one based on principle, I emphasized that objection, though in my own mind the other was the more vital and more compelling.

The points of difference relating to the League of Nations between the President's views and mine, other than the recognition of the primacy of the Great Powers, the affirmative guaranty and the resulting denial in fact of the equality of nations in times of peace, were the provisions in the President's original draft of the Covenant relating to international arbitrations, the subordination of the judicial power to the political power, and the proposed system of mandates. Having discussed with sufficient detail the reasons which caused me to oppose these provisions, and having stated the efforts made to induce President Wilson to abandon or modify them, repetition would be superfluous. It is also needless, in view of the full narrative of events contained in these pages, to state that I failed entirely in my endeavor to divert the President from his determination to have these provisions inserted in the Covenant, except in the case of international arbitrations, and even in that case I do not believe that my advice had anything to do with his abandonment of his ideas as to the method of selecting arbitrators and the right of appeal from arbitral awards. Those changes and the substitution of an article providing for the future creation of a Permanent Court of International Justice, were, in my opinion, as I have said, a concession to the European statesmen and due to their insistence.

President Wilson knew that I disagreed with him as to the relative importance of restoring a state of peace at the earliest date possible and of securing the adoption of a plan for the creation of a League of Nations. He was clearly convinced that the drafting and acceptance of the Covenant was superior to every other task imposed on the Conference, that it must be done before any other settlement was reached and that it ought to have precedence in the negotiations. His course of action was conclusive evidence of this conviction.

On the other hand, I favored the speedy negotiation of a short and simple preliminary treaty, in which, so far as the League of Nations was concerned, there would be a series of declarations and an agreement for a future international conference called for the purpose of drafting a convention in harmony with the declarations in the preliminary treaty. By adopting this course a state of peace would have been restored in the early months of 1919, official intercourse and commercial relations would have been resumed, the more complex and difficult problems of settlement would have been postponed to the negotiation of the definitive Treaty of Peace, and there would have been time to study exhaustively the purposes, powers, and practical operations of a League before the organic agreement was put into final form. Postponement would also have given opportunity to the nations, which had continued neutral throughout the war, to participate in the formation of the plan for a League on an equal footing with the nations which had been belligerents. In the establishment of a world organization universality of international representation in reaching an agreement seemed to me advisable, if not essential, provided the nations represented were democracies and not autocracies.

It was to be presumed also that at a conference entirely independent of the peace negotiations and free from the influences affecting the terms of peace, there would be more general and more frank discussions regarding the various phases of the subject than was possible at a conference ruled by the Five Great Powers and dominated in its decisions, if not in its opinions, by the statesmen of those Powers.

To perfect such a document, as the Covenant of the League of Nations was intended to be, required expert knowledge, practical experience in international relations, and an exchange of ideas untrammeled by immediate questions of policy or by the prejudices resulting from the war and from national hatreds and jealousies. It was not a work for politicians, novices, or inexperienced theorists, but for trained statesmen and jurists, who were conversant with the fundamental principles of international law, with the usages of nations in their intercourse with one another, and with the successes and failures of previous experiments in international association. The President was right in his conception as to the greatness of the task to be accomplished, but he was wrong, radically wrong, in believing that it could be properly done at the Paris Conference under the conditions which there prevailed and in the time given for consideration of the subject.

To believe for a moment that a world constitution — for so its advocates looked upon the Covenant — could be drafted perfectly or even wisely in eleven days, however much thought individuals may have previously given to the subject, seems on the face of it to show an utter lack of appreciation of the problems to be solved or else an abnormal confidence in the talents and wisdom of those charged with the duty. If one compares the learned and comprehensive debates that took place in the convention which drafted the Constitution of the United States, and the months that were spent in the critical examination word by word of the proposed articles, with the ten meetings of the Commission on the League of Nations prior to its report of February 14 and with the few hours given to debating the substance and language of the Covenant, the inferior character of the document produced by the Commission ought not to be a matter of wonder. It was a foregone conclusion that it would be found defective. Some of these defects were subsequently corrected, but the theory and basic principles, which were the chief defects in the plan, were preserved with no substantial change.

But the fact, which has been repeatedly asserted in the preceding pages and which cannot be too strongly emphasized by repetition, is that the most potent and most compelling reason for postponing the consideration of a detailed plan for an international organization was that such a consideration at the outset of the negotiations at Paris obstructed and delayed the discussion and settlement of the general terms necessary to the immediate restoration of a state of peace. Those who recall the political and social conditions in Europe during the winter of 1918–19, to which reference has already been made, will comprehend the apprehension caused by anything which interrupted the negotiation of the peace. No one dared to prophesy what might happen if the state of political uncertainty and industrial stagnation, which existed under the armistices, continued.

The time given to the formulation of the Covenant of the League of Nations and the determination that it should have first place in the negotiations caused such a delay in the proceedings and prevented a speedy restoration of peace. Denial of this is useless. It is too manifest to require proof or argument to support it. It is equally true, I regret to say, that President Wilson was chiefly responsible for this. If he had not insisted that a complete and detailed plan for the League should be part of the treaty negotiated at Paris, and if he had not also insisted that the Covenant be taken up and settled in terms before other matters were considered, a preliminary treaty of peace would in all probability have been signed, ratified, and in effect during April, 1919.

Whatever evils resulted from the failure of the Paris Conference to negotiate promptly a preliminary treaty — and it must be admitted they were not a few — must be credited to those who caused the delay. The personal interviews and secret conclaves before the Commission on the League of Nations met occupied a month and a half. Practically another half month was consumed in sessions of the Commission. The month following was spent by President Wilson on his visit to the United States explaining the reported Covenant and listening to criticisms. While much was done during his absence toward the settlement of numerous questions, final decision in every case awaited his return to Paris. After his arrival the Commission on the League renewed its sittings to consider amendments to its report, and it required over a month to put it in final form for adoption; but during this latter period much time was given to the actual terms of peace, which on account of the delay caused in attempting to perfect the Covenant had taken the form of a definitive rather than a preliminary treaty.

It is conservative to say that between two and three months were spent in the drafting of a document which in the end was rejected by the Senate of the United States and was responsible for the non-ratification of the Treaty of Versailles. In view of the warnings that President Wilson had received as to the probable result of insisting on the plan of a League which he had prepared and his failure to heed the warnings, his persistency in pressing for acceptance of the Covenant before anything else was done makes the resulting delay in the peace less excusable.

Two weeks after the President returned from the United States in March the common opinion was that the drafting of the Covenant had delayed the restoration of peace, an opinion which was endorsed in the press of many countries. The belief became so general and aroused so much popular condemnation that Mr. Wilson considered it necessary to make a public denial, in which he expressed surprise at the published views and declared that the negotiations in regard to the League of Nations had in no way delayed the peace. Concerning the denial and the subject with which it dealt, I made on March 28 the following memorandum:

"The President has issued a public statement, which appears in this morning's papers, in which he refers to the 'surprising impression' that the discussions concerning the League of Nations have delayed the making of peace and he flatly denies that the impression is justified.

"I doubt if this statement will remove the general impression which amounts almost to a conviction. Every one knows that the President's thoughts and a great deal of his time prior to his departure for the United States were given to the formulation of the plan for a League and that he insisted that the 'Covenant' should be drafted and reported before the other features of the peace were considered. The *real* difficulties of the present situation, which had to be settled before the treaty could be drafted, were postponed until his return here on March 13th.

"In fact the real bases of peace have only just begun to receive the attention which they deserve.

"If such questions as the Rhine Provinces, Poland, reparations, and economic arrangements had been taken up by the President and Premiers in January, and if they had sat day and night, as they are now sitting *in camera*, until each was settled, the peace treaty would, I believe, be to-day on the Conference's table, if not actually signed.

"Of course the insistence that the plan of the League be first pushed to a draft before all else prevented the settlement of the other questions. Why attempt to refute what is manifestly true? I regret that the President made the statement because I do not think that it carries conviction. I fear that it will invite controversy and denial, and that it puts the President on the defensive."

The views expressed in this memorandum were those held, I believe, by the great majority of persons who participated in the Peace Conference or were in intimate touch with its proceedings. Mr. Wilson's published denial may have converted some to the belief that the drafting of the Covenant was in no way responsible for the delay of the peace, but the number of converts must have been very few, as it meant utter ignorance of or indifference to the circumstances which conclusively proved the incorrectness of the statement.

The effect of this attempt of President Wilson to check the growing popular antipathy to the League as an obstacle to the speedy restoration of peace was to cause speculation as to whether he really appreciated the situation. If he did not, it was affirmed that he was ignorant of public opinion or else was lacking in mental acuteness. If he did appreciate the state of affairs, it was said that his statement was uttered with the sole purpose of deceiving the people. In either case he fell in public estimation. It shows the unwisdom of having issued the denial.

CHAPTER XV
THE PROPOSED TREATY WITH FRANCE

THERE is one subject, connected with the consideration of the mutual guaranty which, as finally reported by the Commission on the League of Nations, appears as Article 10 of the Covenant, that should be briefly reviewed, as it directly bears upon the value placed upon the guaranty by the French statesmen who accepted it. I refer to the treaties negotiated by France with the United States and Great Britain respectively. These treaties provided that, in the event of France being again attacked by Germany without provocation, the two Powers severally agreed to come to the aid of the French Republic in repelling the invasion. The joint nature of the undertaking was in a provision in each treaty that a similar treaty would be signed by the other Power, otherwise the agreement failed. The undertakings stated in practically identical terms in the two treaties constituted, in fact, a triple defensive alliance for the preservation of the integrity of French territory and French independence. It had the same object as the guaranty in the Covenant, though it went even further in the assurance of affirmative action, and was, therefore, open to the same objections on the grounds of constitutionality and policy as Article 10.

In a note, dated March 20, stating my "Impressions as

to the Present Situation," I discussed the endeavors being made by the President to overcome opposition and to remove obstacles to the acceptance of his plan for a League of Nations by means of compromises and concessions. In the note appears the following:

" An instance of the lengths to which these compromises and makeshifts are going, occurred this morning when Colonel House sent to Mr. White, General Bliss, and me for our opinion the following proposal: That the United States, Great Britain, and France enter into a formal alliance to resist any aggressive action by Germany against France or Belgium, and to employ their military, financial, and economic resources for this purpose in addition to exerting their moral influence to prevent such aggression.

"We three agreed that, if that agreement was made, the chief reason for a League of Nations, as now planned, disappeared. So far as France and Belgium were concerned the alliance was all they needed for their future safety. They might or might not accept the League. Of course they would if the alliance depended upon their acceptance. They would do most anything to get such an alliance.

"The proposal was doubtless made to remove two provisions on which the French are most insistent: *First*, an international military staff to be prepared to use force against Germany if there were signs of military activity; *second*, the creation of an independent Rhenish Republic to act as a 'buffer' state. Of course the triple alliance would make these measures needless.

"What impressed me most was that to gain French support for the League the proposer of the alliance was willing to destroy the chief feature of the League. It seemed to me that here was utter blindness as to the consequences of such action. There appears to have been no thought given as to the way other nations, like Poland, Bohemia, and the Southern Slavs, would view the formation of an alliance to protect France and Belgium alone. Manifestly it would increase rather than decrease their danger from Germany since she would have to look eastward and southward for expansion. Of course they would not accept as sufficient the guaranty in the Covenant when France and Belgium declined to do it.

"How would such a proposal be received in the United States with its traditional policy of avoiding 'entangling alliances'? Of course, when one considers it, the proposal is preposterous and would be laughed at and rejected."

This was the impression made upon me at the time that this triple alliance against Germany was first proposed. I later came to look upon it more seriously and to recognize the fact that there were some valid reasons in favor of the proposal. The subject was not further discussed by the Commissioners for several weeks, but it is clear from what followed that M. Clemenceau, who naturally favored the idea, continued to press the President to agree to the plan. What arguments were employed to persuade him I cannot say, but, knowing the shrewdness of the French Premier in taking advantage of a situation, my belief is that he threatened to withdraw or at least gave the impression that he would withdraw his support of the League of Nations or else would insist on a provision in the Covenant creating a general staff and an international military force and on a provision in the treaty establishing a Rhenish Republic or else ceding to France all territory west of the Rhine. To avoid the adoption of either of these provi-

THE PROPOSED TREATY WITH FRANCE 181

sions, which would have endangered the approval of his plan for world organization, the President submitted to the French demand. At least I assume that was the reason, for he promised to enter into the treaty of assistance which M. Clemenceau insisted should be signed.

It is of course possible that he was influenced in his decision by the belief that the knowledge that such an agreement existed would be sufficient to deter Germany from even planning another invasion of France, but my opinion is that the desire to win French support for the Covenant was the chief reason for the promise that he gave. It should be remembered that at the time both the Italians and Japanese were threatening to make trouble unless their territorial ambitions were satisfied. With these two Powers disaffected and showing a disposition to refuse to accept membership in the proposed League of Nations the opposition of France to the Covenant would have been fatal. It would have been the end of the President's dream of a world organized to maintain peace by an international guaranty of national boundaries and sovereignties. Whether France would in the end have insisted on the additional guaranty of protection I doubt, but it is evident that Mr. Wilson believed that she would and decided to prevent a disaster to his plan by acceding to the wishes of his French colleague.

Some time in April prior to the acceptance of the Treaty of Peace by the Premiers of the Allied Powers, the President and Mr. Lloyd George agreed with M. Clemenceau to negotiate the treaties of protective alliance which the French demanded. The President advised me of his decision on the day before the Treaty was delivered to the German plenipotentiaries stating in substance that his promise to enter into the alliance formed a part of the settlements as fully as if written into the Treaty. I told him that personally I considered an agreement to negotiate the treaty of assistance a mistake, as it discredited Article 10 of the Covenant, which he considered all-important, and as it would, I was convinced, be the cause of serious opposition in the United States. He replied that he considered it necessary to adopt this policy in the circumstances, and that, at any rate, having passed his word with M. Clemenceau, who was accepting the Treaty because of his promise, it was too late to reconsider the matter and useless to discuss it.

Subsequently the President instructed me to have a treaty drafted in accordance with a memorandum which he sent me. This was done by Dr. James Brown Scott and the draft was approved and prepared for signature. On the morning of June 28, the same day on which the Treaty of Versailles was signed, the protective treaty with France was signed at the President's residence in the Place des États Unis by M. Clemenceau and M. Pichon for the French Republic and by President Wilson and myself for the United States, Mr. Lloyd George and Mr. Balfour signing at the same time a similar treaty for Great Britain. Though disagreeing with the policy of the President in

WOODROW WILSON

President of the United States of America

To all to whom these presents shall come, Greetings:

Know ye, That reposing full faith and confidence in the integrity and ability of Robert Lansing, Secretary of State of the United States, I do hereby invest him with full and all manner of power and authority, for and in the name of the United States, to meet and confer with any person or persons invested with like power and authority on the part of France and with him or them to negotiate, conclude and sign a Treaty of assistance to France in the event of unprovoked aggression by Germany, the same to be submitted to the President of the United States for transmission by him to the Senate thereof to receive the advice and consent of that body to its ratification.

IN WITNESS WHEREOF I have hereto set my hand and caused the Seal of the United States to be affixed, this twenty-seventh day of June, in the year of our Lord, one thousand nine hundred and nineteen and of the Independence of the United States of America the 143rd.

Woodrow Wilson

By the President.

Robert Lansing

Secretary of State.

regard to this special treaty it would have been futile for me to have refused to accept the full powers issued to me on June 27 or to have declined to follow the directions to act as a plenipotentiary in signing the document. Such a course would not have prevented Mr. Wilson from entering into the defensive alliance with France and Great Britain and might have actually delayed the peace. Feeling strongly the supreme necessity of ending the existing state of war as soon as possible I did not consider that I would be justified in refusing to act as the formal agent of the President or in disobeying his instructions as such agent. In view of the long delay in ratification of the Treaty of the Peace, I have since doubted whether I acted wisely. But at the time I was convinced that the right course was the one which I followed.

In spite of the fact that my judgment was contrary to the President's as to the wisdom of negotiating this treaty because I considered the policy of doing so bad from the standpoint of national interests and of doubtful expediency in view of the almost certain rejection of it by the United States Senate and of its probable effect on any plan for general disarmament, I was not entirely satisfied because I could not disregard the fact that an argument could be made in its favor which was not without force.

The United States entered the war to check the progress of the autocratic imperialism of Germany. That purpose became generally recognized before the victory was won. In making peace it was deemed, therefore, a matter of first importance to make impossible a revival of the aggressive spirit and ambitious designs of Germany. The prevailing bitterness against France because of the territorial cessions and the reparations demanded by the victor would naturally cause the German people to seek future opportunity to be revenged. With a population almost, if not quite, double that of the French Republic, Germany would be a constant menace to the nation which had suffered so terribly in the past by reason of the imperialistic spirit prevalent in the German Empire. The fear of that menace strongly influenced the French policies during the negotiations at Paris. In fact it was hard to avoid the feeling that this fear dominated the conduct of the French delegates and the attitude of their Government. They demanded much, and recognizing the probable effect of their demands on the German people sought to obtain special protection in case their vanquished enemy attempted in the future to dispossess them by force of the land which he had been compelled to surrender or attempted to make them restore the indemnity paid.

Whether France could have avoided the danger of German attack in the future by lessening her demands, however just they might be, is neither here nor there. It makes little practical difference how that question is answered. The important fact is that the settlements in favor of France under the Treaty were of a nature which made the continuance of peace between the two nations doubtful if Germany possessed the ability to regain her military strength and if nothing was done to prevent her from using it. In these circumstances a special protective treaty seemed a practical way to check the conversion of the revengeful spirit of the Germans into another war of invasion.

However valid this argument in favor of the two treaties of assistance, and though my personal sympathy for France inclined me to satisfy her wishes, my judgment, as an American Commissioner, was that American interests and the traditional policies of the United States were against this alliance. Possibly the President recognized the force of the argument in favor of the treaty and valued it so highly that he considered it decisive. Knowing, however, his general attitude toward French demands and his confidence in the effectiveness of the guaranty in the Covenant, I believe that the controlling reason for promising the alliance and negotiating the treaty was his conviction that it was necessary to make this concession to the French in order to secure their support for the Covenant and to check the disposition in certain quarters to make the League of Nations essentially a military coalition under a general international staff organized and controlled by the French.

There were those who favored the mutual guaranty in the Covenant, but who strongly opposed the separate treaty with France. Their objection was that, in view of the general guaranty, the treaty of assistance was superfluous, or, if it were considered necessary, then it discredited the Covenant's guaranty. The argument was logical and difficult to controvert. It was the one taken by delegates of the smaller nations who relied on the general guaranty to protect their countries from future aggressions on the part of their powerful neighbors. If the guaranty of the Covenant was sufficient protection for them, they declared that it ought to be sufficient for France. If France doubted its sufficiency, how could they be content with it?

Since my own judgment was against any form of guaranty imposing upon the United States either a legal or a moral obligation to employ coercive measures under certain conditions arising in international affairs, I could not conscientiously support the idea of the French treaty. This further departure from America's historic policy caused me to accept President Wilson's "guidance and direction . . . with increasing reluctance," as he aptly expressed it in his letter of February 11, 1920. We did not agree, we could not agree, since our points of view were so much at variance.

Yet, in spite of the divergence of our views as to the negotiations which constantly increased and became more and more pronounced during the six months at Paris, our personal relations continued unchanged; at least there was no outward evidence of the actual breach which existed. As there never had been the personal intimacy between the President and myself, such as existed in the case of Colonel House and a few others of his advisers, and as our intercourse had always been more or less formal in character, it was easier to continue the official relations that had previously prevailed. I presume that Mr. Wilson felt, as I did, that it would create an embarrassing situation in the negotiations if there was an open rupture between us or if my commission was withdrawn or surrendered and I returned to the United States before the Treaty of Peace was signed. The effect, too, upon the situation in the Senate would be to strengthen the opposition to the President's purposes and furnish his personal, as well as his political, enemies with new grounds for attacking him.

I think, however, that our reasons for avoiding a public break in our official relations were different. The President undoubtedly believed that such an event would jeopardize the acceptance of the Covenant by the United States Senate in view of the hostility to it which had already developed and which was supplemented by the bitter animosity to him personally which was undisguised. On my part, the chief reason for leaving the situation undisturbed was that I was fully convinced that my withdrawal from the American Commission would seriously delay the restoration of peace, possibly in the signature of the Treaty at Paris and certainly in its ratification at Washington. Considering that the time had passed to make an attempt to change Mr. Wilson's views on any fundamental principle, and believing it a duty to place no obstacle in the way of the signature and ratification of the Treaty of Peace with Germany, I felt that there was no course for me as a representative of the United States other than to obey the President's orders however strong my personal inclination might be to refuse to follow a line of action which seemed to me wrong in principle and unwise in policy.

In view of the subsequent contest between the President and the opposition Senators over the Treaty of Versailles, resulting in its non-ratification and the consequent delay in the restoration of a state of peace between the United States and Germany, my failure at Paris to decline to follow the President may be open to criticism, if not to censure. But it can hardly be considered just to pass judgment on my conduct by what occurred after the signature of the Treaty unless what would occur was a foregone conclusion, and at that time it was not even suggested that the Treaty would fail of ratification. The decision had to be made under the conditions and expectations which then prevailed. Unquestionably there was on June 28, 1919, a common belief that the President would compose his differences with a sufficient number of the Republican Senators to obtain the necessary consent of two thirds of the Senate to the ratification of the Treaty, and that the delay in senatorial action would be brief. I personally believed that that would be the result, although Mr. Wilson's experience in Washington in February and the rigid attitude, which he then assumed, might have been a warning as to the future. Seeing the situation as I did, no man would have been willing to imperil immediate ratification by resigning as Commissioner on the ground that he was opposed to the President's policies. A return to peace was at stake, and peace was the supreme need of the world, the universal appeal of all peoples. I could not conscientiously assume the responsibility of placing any obstacle in the way of a return to peace at the earliest possible moment. It would have been to do the very thing which I condemned in the President when he prevented an early signing of the peace by insisting on the acceptance of the Covenant of the League of Nations as a condition precedent. Whatever the consequence of my action would have been, whether it resulted in delay or in defeat of ratification, I should have felt guilty of having prevented an immediate peace which from the first seemed to me vitally important to all nations. Personal feelings and even personal beliefs were insufficient to excuse such action.

CHAPTER XVI

LACK OF AN AMERICAN PROGRAMME

HAVING reviewed the radical differences between the President and myself in regard to the League of Nations and the inclusion of the Covenant in the Treaty of Peace with Germany, it is necessary to revert to the early days of the negotiations at Paris in order to explain the divergence of our views as to the necessity of a definite programme for the American Commission to direct it in its work and to guide its members in their intercourse with the delegates of other countries.

If the President had a programme, other than the general principles and the few territorial settlements included in his Fourteen Points, and the generalities contained in his "subsequent addresses," he did not show a copy of the programme to the Commissioners or advise them of its contents. The natural conclusion was that he had never worked out in detail the application of his announced principles or put into concrete form the specific settlements which he had declared ought to be in the terms of peace. The definition of the principles, the interpretation of the policies, and the detailing of the provisions regarding territorial settlements were not apparently attempted by Mr. Wilson. They were in large measure left uncertain by the phrases in which they were delivered. Without authoritative explanation, interpretation, or application to actual facts they formed incomplete and inadequate instructions to Commissioners who were authorized "to negotiate peace."

An examination of the familiar Fourteen Points uttered by the President in his address of January 8, 1918, will indicate the character of the declarations, which may be, by reason of their thought and expression, termed "Wilsonian" (Appendix IV, p. 314). The first five Points are announcements of principle which should govern the peace negotiations. The succeeding eight Points refer to territorial adjustments, but make no attempt to define actual boundaries, so essential in conducting negotiations regarding territory. The Fourteenth Point relates to the formation of " a general association of the nations for the purpose of affording mutual guarantees of political independence and territorial integrity to great and small nations alike."

It is hardly worth while to say that the Fourteen Points and the four principles declared in the address of February 11, 1918 (Appendix V, p. 317), do not constitute a sufficient programme for negotiators. Manifestly they are too indefinite in specific application. They were never intended for that purpose when they were proclaimed. They might have formed a general basis for the preparation of instructions for peace commissioners, but they omitted too many of the essentials to be considered actual instructions, while the lack of definite terms to be included in a treaty further deprived them of that character. Such important and practical subjects as reparations, financial arrangements, the use and control of waterways, and other questions of a like nature, are not even mentioned. As a general statement of the bases of peace the Fourteen Points and subsequent declarations probably served a useful purpose, though some critics would deny it, but as a working programme for the negotiation of a treaty they were inadequate, if not wholly useless.

Believing in the autumn of 1918 that the end of the war was approaching and assuming that the American plenipotentiaries to the Peace Conference would have to be furnished with detailed written instructions as to the terms of the treaty to be signed, I prepared on September 21, 1918, a memorandum of my views as to the territorial settlements which would form, not instructions, but a guide in the drafting of instructions for the American Commissioners. At the time I had no intimation that the President purposed to be present in person at the peace table and had not even thought of such a possibility. The memorandum, which follows, was written with the sole purpose of being ready to draft definite instructions which could be submitted to the President when the time came to prepare for the negotiation of the peace. The memorandum follows:

"The present Russian situation, which is unspeakably horrible and which seems beyond present hope of betterment, presents new problems to be solved at the peace table.

"The Pan-Germans now have in shattered and impotent Russia the opportunity to develop an alternative or supplemental scheme to their 'Mittel-Europa' project. German domination over Southern Russia would offer as advantageous, if not a more advantageous, route to the Persian Gulf than through the turbulent Balkans and unreliable Turkey. If both routes, north and south of the Black Sea, could be controlled, the Pan-Germans would have gained more than they dreamed of obtaining. I believe, however, that Bulgaria fears the Germans and will be disposed to resist German domination possibly to the extent of making a separate peace with the Allies. Nevertheless, if the Germans could obtain the route north of the Black Sea, they would with reason consider the war a successful venture because it would give them the opportunity to rebuild the imperial power and to carry out the Prussian ambition of world-mastery.

"The treaty of peace must not leave Germany in possession directly or indirectly of either of these routes to the Orient. There must be territorial barriers erected to prevent that Empire from ever being able by political or economic penetration to become dominant in those regions.

"With this in view I would state the essentials for a stable peace as follows, though I do so in the most tentative way because conditions may change materially. These 'essentials' relate to territory and waters, and do not deal with military protection.

"*First.* The complete abrogation or denouncement of the Brest-Litovsk Treaty and all treaties relating in any way to Russian territory or commerce; and also the same action as to the Treaty of Bucharest. This applies to all treaties made by the German Empire or Germany's allies.

"*Second.* The Baltic Provinces of Lithuania, Latvia, and Esthonia should be autonomous states of a Russian Confederation.

"*Third.* Finland raises a different question and it should

be carefully considered whether it should not be an independent state.

"*Fourth.* An independent Poland, composed of Polish provinces of Russia, Prussia, and Austria, and in possession of the port of Danzig.

"*Fifth.* An independent state, either single or federal composed of Bohemia, Slovakia, and Moravia (and possibly a portion of Silesia) and possessing an international right of way by land or water to a free port.

"*Sixth.* The Ukraine to be a state of the Russian Confederation, to which should be annexed that portion of the Austro-Hungarian Empire in which the Ruthenians predominate.

"*Seventh.* Roumania, in addition to her former territory, should ultimately be given sovereignty over Bessarabia, Transylvania, and the upper portion of the Dobrudja, leaving the central mouth of the Danube as the boundary of Bulgaria, or else the northern half. (As to the boundary there is doubt.)

"*Eighth.* The territories in which the Jugo-Slavs predominate, namely Croatia, Slavonia, Dalmatia, Bosnia, and Herzegovina, should be united with Serbia and Montenegro forming a single or a federal state. The sovereignty over Trieste or some other port should be later settled in drawing a boundary line between the new state and Italy. My present view is that there should be a good Jugo-Slav port.

"*Ninth.* Hungary should be separated from Austria and possess rights of free navigation of the Danube.

"*Tenth.* Restoration to Italy of all the Italian provinces of Austria. Italy's territory to extend along the northern Adriatic shore to the Jugo-Slav boundary. Certain ports on the eastern side of the Adriatic should be considered as possible naval bases of Italy. (This last is doubtful.)

"*Eleventh*. Reduction of Austria to the ancient boundaries and title of the Archduchy of Austria. Incorporation of Archduchy in the Imperial German Confederation. Austrian outlet to the sea would be like that of Baden and Saxony through German ports on the North Sea and the Baltic.

"*Twelfth*. The boundaries of Bulgaria, Serbia, and Greece to follow in general those established after the First Balkan War, though Bulgaria should surrender to Greece more of the Ægean coast and obtain the southern half only of the Dobrudja (or else as far as the Danube) and the Turkish territory up to the district surrounding Constantinople, to be subsequently decided upon.

"*Thirteenth*. Albania to be under Italian or Serbian sovereignty or incorporated in the Jugo-Slav Confederation.

"*Fourteenth*. Greece to obtain more of the Ægean litoral at the expense of Bulgaria, the Greek-inhabited islands adjacent to Asia Minor and possibly certain ports and adjoining territory in Asia Minor.

"*Fifteenth*. The Ottoman Empire to be reduced to Anatolia and have no possessions in Europe. (This requires consideration.)

"*Sixteenth*. Constantinople to be erected into an international protectorate surrounded by a land zone to allow for expansion of population. The form of government to be determined upon by an international commission or by one Government acting as the mandatory of the Powers. The commission or mandatory to have the regulation and control of the navigation of the Dardanelles and Bosphorus as international waterways.

"*Seventeenth*. Armenia and Syria to be erected into protectorates of such Government or Governments as seems expedient from a domestic as well as an international point of view; the guaranty being that both countries will be given self-government as soon as possible and that an 'Open-Door' policy as to commerce and industrial development will be rigidly observed.

"*Eighteenth.* Palestine to be an autonomous state under a general international protectorate or under the protectorate of a Power designated to act as the mandatory of the Powers.

"*Nineteenth.* Arabia to receive careful consideration as to the full or partial sovereignty of the state or states established.

"*Twentieth.* Great Britain to have the sovereignty of Egypt, or a full protectorate over it.

"*Twenty-first.* Persia to be freed from all treaties establishing spheres of influence. Rigid application of the 'Open-Door' policy in regard to commercial and industrial development.

"*Twenty-second.* All Alsace-Lorraine to be restored to France without conditions.

"*Twenty-third.* Belgium to be restored to full sovereignty.

"*Twenty-fourth.* A consideration of the union of Luxemburg to Belgium. (This is open to question.)

"*Twenty-fifth.* The Kiel Canal to be internationalized and an international zone twenty miles from the Canal on either side to be erected which should be, with the Canal, under the control and regulation of Denmark as the mandatory of the Powers. (This last is doubtful.)

"*Twenty-sixth.* All land north of the Kiel Canal Zone to be ceded to Denmark.

"*Twenty-seventh.* The fortifications of the Kiel Canal and of Heligoland to be dismantled. Heligoland to be ceded to Denmark.

"*Twenty-eighth.* The sovereignty of the archipelago of Spitzbergen to be granted to Norway.

"*Twenty-ninth.* The disposition of the colonial possessions formerly belonging to Germany to be determined by an international commission having in mind the interests of the inhabitants and the possibility of employing these colonies as a means of indemnification for wrongs done. The 'Open-Door' policy should be guaranteed.

"While the foregoing definitive statement as to territory contains my views at the present time (September 21, 1918), I feel that no proposition should be considered unalterable, as further study and conditions which have not been disclosed may materially change some of them.

"Three things must constantly be kept in mind, the natural stability of race, language, and nationality, the necessity of every nation having an outlet to the sea so that it may maintain its own merchant marine, and the imperative need of rendering Germany impotent as a military power."

Later I realized that another factor should be given as important a place in the terms of peace as any of the three, namely, the economic interdependence of adjoining areas and the mutual industrial benefit to their inhabitants by close political affiliation. This factor in the territorial settlements made more and more impression upon me as it was disclosed by a detailed study of the numerous problems which the Peace Conference had to solve.

I made other memoranda on various subjects relating to the general peace for the purpose of crystallizing my ideas, so that I could lay them in concrete form before the President when the time came to draft instructions for the American plenipotentiaries charged with the negotiation of the Treaty of Peace. When the President reached the decision to attend the Conference and to direct in person the negotiations, it became evident that, in place of the instructions customarily issued to negotiators, a more practical and proper form of defining the objects to be sought by the United States would be an outline of a treaty setting forth in detail the features of the peace, or else a memorandum containing definite declarations of policy in regard to the numerous problems presented. Unless there was some framework of this sort on which to build, it would manifestly be very embarrassing for the American Commissioners in their intercourse with their foreign colleagues, as they would be unable to discuss authoritatively or even informally the questions at issue or express opinions upon them without the danger of unwittingly opposing the President's wishes or of contradicting the views which might be expressed by some other of their associates on the American Commission. A definite plan seemed essential if the Americans were to take any part in the personal exchanges of views which are so usual during the progress of negotiations.

Prior to the departure of the American delegation from the United States and for two weeks after their arrival in Paris, it was expected that the President would submit to the Commissioners for their guidance a *projet* of a treaty or a very complete programme as to policies. Nothing, however, was done, and in the conferences which took place between the President and his American associates he confined his remarks almost exclusively to the League of Nations and to his plan for its organization. It was evident — at least that was the natural inference — that President Wilson was without a programme of any sort or even of a list of subjects suitable as an outline for the preparation of a programme. How he purposed to conduct the negotiations no one seemed to know. It was all very uncertain and unsatisfactory.

In the circumstances, which seemed to be due to the President's failure to appreciate the necessity for a definite programme, I felt that something ought to be done, as the probable result would be that the terms of the Treaty, other than the provisions regarding a League of Nations, would be drafted by foreign delegates and not by the President.

Impressed by the unsatisfactory state of affairs and desirous of remedying it if possible, I asked Dr. James Brown Scott and Mr. David Hunter Miller, the legal advisers of the American Commission, to prepare a skeleton treaty covering the subjects to be dealt with in the negotiations which could be used in working out a complete programme. After several conferences with these advisers concerning the subjects to be included and their arrangement in the Treaty, the work was sufficiently advanced to lay before the Commissioners. Copies were, therefore, furnished to them with the request that they give the document consideration in order that they might make criticisms and suggest changes. I had not sent a copy to the President, intending to await the views of my colleagues before doing so, but during the conference of January 10, to which I have been compelled reluctantly to refer in discussing the Covenant of the League of Nations, I mentioned the fact that our legal advisers had been for some time at work on a "skeleton treaty" and had made a tentative draft. The President at once showed his displeasure and resented the action taken, evidently considering the request that a draft be prepared to be a usurpation of his authority to direct the activities of the Commission. It was this incident which called forth his remark, to which reference was made in Chapter VIII, that he did not propose to have lawyers drafting the Treaty.

In view of Mr. Wilson's attitude it was useless for Dr. Scott and Mr. Miller to proceed with their outline of a treaty or for the Commissioners to give consideration to the tentative draft already made. It was a disagreeable situation. If the President had had anything, however crude and imperfect it might have been, to submit in place of the Scott-Miller draft, it would have been a different matter and removed to an extent the grounds for complaint at his attitude. But he offered nothing at all as a substitute. It is fair to assume that he had no programme prepared and was unwilling to have any one else make a tentative one for his consideration. It left the American Commission without a chart marking out the course which they were to pursue in the negotiations and apparently without a pilot who knew the channel.

Six days after the enforced abandonment of the plan to prepare a skeleton treaty as a foundation for a definite and detailed programme, I made the following note which expresses my views on the situation at that time:

"*January* 16, 1919

"No plan of work has been prepared. Unless something is done we will be here for many weeks, possibly for months. After the President's remarks the other day about a draft-treaty no one except the President would think of preparing a plan. He must do it himself, and he is not doing it. He has not even given us a list of subjects to be considered and of course has made no division of our labors.

"If the President does not take up this matter of organization and systematically apportion the subjects between us, we may possibly have no peace before June. This would be preposterous because with proper order and division of questions we ought to have a treaty signed by April first.

"I feel as if we, the Commissioners, were like a lot of skilled workmen who are ordered to build a house. We have the materials and tools, but there are no plans and specifications and no master-workman in charge of the construction. We putter around in an aimless sort of way and get nowhere.

"With all his natural capacity the President seems to lack the faculty of employing team-work and of adopting a system to utilize the brains of other men. It is a decided defect in an executive. He would not make a good head of a governmental department. The result is, so far as our Commission is concerned, a state of confusion and uncertainty with a definite loss and delay through effort being undirected. "

On several occasions I spoke to the President about a programme for the work of the Commission and its corps of experts, but he seemed indisposed to consider the subject and gave the impression that he intended to call on the experts for his own information which would be all that was necessary. I knew that Colonel House, through Dr. Mezes, the head of the organization, was directing the preparation of certain data, but whether he was doing so under the President's directions I did not know, though I presumed such was the case. Whatever data were furnished did not, however, pass through the hands of the other Commissioners who met every morning in my office to exchange information and discuss matters pertaining to the negotiations and to direct the routine work of the Commission.

It is difficult, even with the entire record of the proceedings at Paris before one, to find a satisfactory explanation for the President's objection to having a definite programme other than the general declarations contained in the Fourteen Points and his "subsequent addresses." It may be that he was unwilling to bind himself to a fixed programme, since it would restrict him, to an extent, in his freedom of action and prevent him from assuming any position which seemed to him expedient at the time when a question arose during the negotiations. It may be that he did not wish to commit himself in any way to the contents of a treaty until the Covenant of the League of Nations had been accepted. It may be that he preferred not to let the American Commissioners know his views, as they would then be in a position to take an active part in the informal discussions which he apparently wished to handle alone. None of these explanations is at all satisfactory, and yet any one of them may be the true one.

Whatever was the chief reason for the President's failure to furnish a working plan to the American Commissioners, he knowingly adopted the policy and clung to it with the tenacity of purpose which has been one of the qualities of mind that account for his great successes and for his great failures. I use the adverb "knowingly" because it had been made clear to him that, in the judgment of others, the Commissioners ought to have the guidance furnished by a draft-treaty or by a definite statement of policies no matter how tentative or subject to change the draft or statement might be.

On the day that the President left Paris to return to the United States (February 14, 1919) I asked him if he had any instructions for the Commissioners during his absence concerning the settlements which should be included in the preliminary treaty of peace, as it was understood that the Council of Ten would continue its sessions for the consideration of the subjects requiring investigation and decision. The President replied that he had no instructions, that the decisions could wait until he returned, though the hearings could proceed and reports could be made during his absence. Astonished as I was at this wish to delay these matters, I suggested to him the subjects which I thought ought to go into the Treaty. He answered that he did not care to discuss them at that time, which, as he was about to depart from Paris, meant that everything must rest until he had returned from his visit to Washington.

Since I was the head of the American Commission when the President was absent and became the spokesman for the United States on the Council of Ten, this refusal to disclose his views even in a general way placed me in a very awkward position. Without instructions and without knowledge of the President's wishes or purposes the conduct of the negotiations was difficult and progress toward actual settlements practically impossible. As a matter of fact the Council did accomplish a great amount of work, while the President was away, in the collection of data and preparing questions for final settlement. But so far as deciding questions was concerned, which ought to have been the principal duty of the Council of Ten, it simply "marked time," as I had no power to decide or even to express an authoritative opinion on any subject. It showed very clearly that the President intended to do everything himself and to allow no one to act for him unless it was upon some highly technical matter. All actual decisions in regard to the terms of peace which involved policy were thus forced to await his time and pleasure.

Even after Mr. Wilson returned to Paris and resumed his place as head of the American delegation he was apparently without a programme. On March 20, six days after his return, I made a note that "the President, so far as I can judge, has yet no definite programme," and that I was unable to "find that he has talked over a plan of a treaty even with Colonel House." It is needless to quote the thoughts, which I recorded at the time, in regard to the method in which the President was handling a great international negotiation, a method as unusual as it was unwise. I referred to Colonel House's lack of information concerning the President's purposes because he was then and had been from the beginning on more intimate terms with the President than any other American. If he did not know the President's mind, it was safe to assume that no one knew it.

I had, as has been stated, expressed to Mr. Wilson my views as to what the procedure should be and had obtained no action. With the responsibility resting on him for the conduct and success of the negotiations and with his constitutional authority to exercise his own judgment in regard to every matter pertaining to the treaty, there was nothing further to be done in relieving the situation of the American Commissioners from embarrassment or in inducing the President to adopt a better course than the haphazard one that he was pursuing.

It is apparent that we differed radically as to the necessity for a clearly defined programme and equally so as to the advantages to be gained by having a draft-treaty made or a full statement prepared embodying the provisions to be sought by the United States in the negotiations. I did not attempt to hide my disapproval of the vagueness and uncertainty of the President's method, and there is no doubt in my own mind that Mr. Wilson was fully cognizant of my opinion. How far this lack of system in the work of the Commission and the failure to provide a plan for a treaty affected the results written into the Treaty of Versailles is speculative, but my belief is that they impaired in many particulars the character of the settlements by frequent abandonment of principle for the sake of expediency.

The want of a programme or even of an unwritten plan as to the negotiations was further evidenced by the fact that the President, certainly as late as March 19, had not made up his mind whether the treaty which was being negotiated should be preliminary or final. He had up to that time the peculiar idea that a preliminary treaty was in the nature of a *modus vivendi* which could be entered into independently by the Executive and which would restore peace without going through the formalities of senatorial consent to ratification.

The purpose of Mr. Wilson, so far as one could judge, was to include in a preliminary treaty of the sort that he intended to negotiate, the entire Covenant of the League of Nations and other principal settlements, binding the signatories to repeat these provisions in the final and definitive treaty when that was later negotiated. By this method peace would be at once restored, the United States and other nations associated with it in the war would be obligated to renew diplomatic and consular relations with Germany, and commercial intercourse would follow as a matter of course. All this was to be done without going through the American constitutional process of obtaining the advice and consent of the Senate to the Covenant and to the principal settlements. The intent seemed to be to respond to the popular demand for an immediate peace and at the same time to checkmate the opponents of the Covenant in the Senate by having the League of Nations organized and functioning before the definitive treaty was laid before that body.

When the President advanced this extraordinary theory of the nature of a preliminary treaty during a conversation, of which I made a full memorandum, I told him that it was entirely wrong, that by whatever name the document was called, whether it was "armistice," "agreement," "protocol," or "*modus*," it would be a treaty and would have to be sent by him to the Senate for its approval. I said, "If we change the *status* from war to peace, it has to be by a ratified treaty. There is no other way save by a joint resolution of Congress." At this statement the President was evidently much perturbed. He did not accept it as conclusive, for he asked me to obtain the opinion of others on the subject. He was evidently loath to abandon the plan that he had presumably worked out as a means of preventing the Senate from rejecting or modifying the Covenant before it came into actual operation. It seems almost needless to say that all the legal experts, among them Thomas W. Gregory, the retiring Attorney-

General of the United States, who chanced to be in Paris at the time, agreed with my opinion, and upon being so informed the President abandoned his purpose.

It is probable that the conviction, which was forced upon Mr. Wilson, that he could not independently of the Senate put into operation a preliminary treaty, determined him to abandon that type of treaty and to proceed with the negotiation of a definitive one. At least I had by March 30 reached the conclusion that there would be no preliminary treaty as is disclosed by the following memorandum written on that day:

"I am sure now that there will be no preliminary treaty of peace, but that the treaty will be complete and definitive. This is a serious mistake. Time should be given for passions to cool. The operations of a preliminary treaty should be tested and studied. It would hasten a restoration of peace. Certainly this is the wise course as to territorial settlements and the financial and economic burdens to be imposed upon Germany. The same comment applies to the organization of a League of Nations. Unfortunately the President insists on a full-blown Covenant and not a declaration of principles. This has much to do with preventing a preliminary treaty, since he wishes to make the League an agent for enforcement of definite terms.

"When the President departed for the United States in February, I assumed and I am certain that he had in mind that there would be a preliminary treaty. With that in view I drafted at the time a memorandum setting forth what the preliminary treaty of peace should contain. Here are the subjects I then set down:

"1. Restoration of Peace and official relations.

"2. Restoration of commercial and financial relations subject to conditions.

"3. Renunciation by Germany of all territory and territorial rights outside of Europe.

"4. Minimum territory of Germany in Europe, the boundaries to be fixed in the Definitive Treaty.

"5. Maximum military and naval establishments and production of arms and munitions.

"6. Maximum amount of money and property to be surrendered by Germany with time limits for payment and delivery.

"7. German property and territory to be held as security by the Allies until the Definitive Treaty is ratified.

"8. Declaration as to the organization of a League of Nations.

"The President's obsession as to a League of Nations blinds him to everything else. An immediate peace is nothing to him compared to the adoption of the Covenant. The whole world wants peace. The President wants his League. I think that the world will have to wait."

The eight subjects, above stated, were the ones which I called to the President's attention at the time he was leaving Paris for the United States and which he said he did not care to discuss.

The views that are expressed in the memorandum of March 30 are those that I have continued to hold. The President was anxious to have the Treaty, even though preliminary in character, contain detailed rather than general provisions, especially as to the League of Nations. With that view I entirely disagreed, as detailed terms of settlement and the articles of the Covenant as proposed would cause discussion and unquestionably delay the peace. To restore the peaceful intercourse between the belligerents, to open the long-closed channels of commerce, and to give to the war-stricken peoples of Europe opportunity to resume their normal industrial life seemed to me the first and greatest task to be accomplished. It was in my judgment superior to every other object of the Paris negotiations. Compared with it the creation of a League of Nations was insignificant and could well be postponed. President Wilson thought otherwise. We were very far apart in this matter as he well knew, and he rightly assumed that I followed his instructions with reluctance, and, he might have added, with grave concern.

As a matter of interest in this connection and as a possible source from which the President may have acquired knowledge of my views as to the conduct of the negotiations, I would call attention again to the conference which I had with Colonel House on December 17, 1918, and to which I have referred in connection with the subject of international arbitration. During that conference I said to the Colonel "that I thought that there ought to be a preliminary treaty of peace negotiated without delay, and that all the details as to a League of Nations, boundaries, and indemnities should wait for the time being. The Colonel replied that he was not so sure about delaying the creation of a League, as he was afraid that it never could be put through unless it was done at once. I told him that possibly he was right, but that I was opposed to anything which delayed the peace." This quotation is from my memorandum made at the time of our conversation. I think that the same reason for insisting on negotiating the Covenant largely influenced the course of the President. My impression at the time was that the Colonel favored a preliminary treaty provided that there was included in it the full plan for a League of Nations, which to me seemed to be impracticable.

There can be little doubt that, if there had been a settled programme prepared or a tentative treaty drafted, there would have been a preliminary treaty which might and probably would have postponed the negotiations as to a League. Possibly the President realized that this danger of excluding the Covenant existed and for that reason was unwilling to make a definite programme or to let a draft-treaty be drawn. At least it may have added another reason for his proceeding without advising the Commissioners of his purposes.

As I review the entire negotiations and the incidents which took place at Paris, President Wilson's inherent dislike to depart in the least from an announced course, a characteristic already referred to, seems to me to have been the most potent influence in determining his method of work during the Peace Conference. He seemed to think that, having marked out a definite plan of action, any deviation from it would show intellectual weakness or vacillation of purpose. Even when there could be no doubt that in view of changed conditions it was wise to change a policy, which he had openly adopted or approved, he clung to it with peculiar tenacity refusing or merely failing to modify it. Mr. Wilson's mind once made up seemed to become inflexible. It appeared to grow impervious to arguments and even to facts. It lacked the elasticity and receptivity which have always been characteristic of sound judgment and right thinking. He might break, but he would not bend. This rigidity of mind accounts in large measure for the deplorable, and, as it seemed to me, needless, conflict between the President and the Senate over the Treaty of Versailles. It accounts for other incidents in his career which have materially weakened his influence and cast doubts on his wisdom. It also accounts, in my opinion, for the President's failure to prepare or to adopt a programme at Paris or to commit himself to a draft of a treaty as a basis for the negotiations, which failure, I am convinced, not only prevented the signature of a short preliminary treaty of peace, but lost Mr. Wilson the leadership in the proceedings, as the statesmen of the other Great Powers outlined the Treaty negotiated and suggested the majority of the articles which were written into it. It would have made a vast difference if the President had known definitely what he sought, but he apparently did not. He dealt in generalities leaving, but not committing, to others their definition and application. He was always in the position of being able to repudiate the interpretation which others might place upon his declarations of principle.

CHAPTER XVII
SECRET DIPLOMACY

ANOTHER matter, concerning which the President and I disagreed, was the secrecy with which the negotiations were carried on between him and the principal European statesmen, incidental to which was the willingness, if not the desire, to prevent the proceedings and decisions from becoming known even to the delegates of the smaller nations which were represented at the Peace Conference.

Confidential personal interviews were to a certain extent unavoidable and necessary, but to conduct the entire negotiation through a small group sitting behind closed doors and to shroud their proceedings with mystery and uncertainty made a very unfortunate impression on those who were not members of the secret councils.

At the first there was no Council of the Heads of States (the so-called Council of Four); in fact it was not recognized as an organized body until the latter part of March, 1919. Prior to that time the directing body of the Conference was the self-constituted Council of Ten composed of the President and the British, French, and Italian Premiers with their Secretaries or Ministers of Foreign Affairs, and two Japanese delegates of ambassadorial rank. This Council had a membership identical with that of the Supreme War Council, which controlled the armistices, their enforcement, and other military matters. It assumed authority over the negotiations and proceedings of the Conference, though it was never authorized so to do by the body of delegates. The Council of Four, when later formed, was equally without a mandate from the Conference. They assumed the authority and exercised it as a matter of right.

From the time of his arrival in Paris President Wilson held almost daily conversations with the leading foreign statesmen. It would be of little value to speculate on what took place at these interviews, since the President seldom told the American Commission of the meetings or disclosed to them, unless possibly to Colonel House, the subjects which were discussed. My conviction is, from the little information which the President volunteered, that these consultations were — certainly at first — devoted to inducing the European leaders to give their support to his plan for a League of Nations, and that, as other matters relating to the terms of peace were in a measure involved because of their possible relation to the functions of the League, they too became more and more subjects of discussion.

The introduction of this personal and clandestine method of negotiation was probably due to the President's belief that he could in this way exercise more effectively his personal influence in favor of the acceptance of a League. It is not unlikely that this belief was in a measure justified. In Colonel House he found one to aid him in this course of procedure, as the Colonel's intimate association with the principal statesmen of the Allied Powers during previous visits to Europe as the President's personal envoy was an asset which he could utilize as an intermediary between the President and those with whom he wished to confer. Mr. Wilson relied upon Colonel House for his knowledge of the views and temperaments of the men with whom he had to deal. It was not strange that he should adopt a method which the Colonel had found successful in the past and that he should seek the latter's aid and advice in connection with the secret conferences which usually took place at the residence of the President.

Mr. Wilson pursued this method of handling the subjects of negotiation the more readily because he was by nature and by inclination secretive. He had always shown a preference for a private interview with an individual. In his conduct of the executive affairs of the Government at Washington he avoided as far as possible general conferences. He talked a good deal about "taking common counsel," but showed no disposition to put it into practice. He followed the same course in the matter of foreign affairs. At Paris this characteristic, which had often been the subject of remark in Washington, was more pronounced, or at least more noticeable. He was not disposed to discuss matters with the American Commission as a whole or even to announce to them his decisions unless something arose which compelled him to do so. He easily fell into the practice of seeing men separately and of keeping secret the knowledge acquired as well as the effect of this knowledge on his views and purposes. To him this was the normal and most satisfactory method of doing business.

From the time that the President arrived in Paris up to the time that the Commission on the League of Nations made its report — that is, from December 14, 1918, to February 14, 1919 — the negotiations regarding the League were conducted with great secrecy. Colonel House, the President's collaborator in drafting the Covenant, if he was not, as many believed, the real author, was the only American with whom Mr. Wilson freely conferred and to whom he confided the progress that he was making in his interviews with the foreign statesmen, at many of which interviews the Colonel was present. It is true that the President held an occasional conference with all the American Commissioners, but these conferences were casual and perfunctory in nature and were very evidently not for the purpose of obtaining the opinions and counsel of the Commissioners. There was none of the frankness that should have existed between the Chief Executive and his chosen agents and advisers. The impression made was that he summoned the conferences to satisfy the *amour propre* of the Commissioners rather than out of any personal wish to do so.

The consequence was that the American Commissioners, other than Colonel House, were kept in almost complete ignorance of the preliminary negotiations and were left to gather such information as they were able from the delegates of other Powers, who, naturally assuming that the Americans possessed the full confidence of the President, spoke with much freedom. As Mr. Wilson never held a conference with the American Commission from the first meeting of the Commission on the League of Nations until its report was printed, his American colleagues did not know, except indirectly, of the questions at issue or of the progress that was being made. The fact is that, as the Commission on the League met in Colonel House's office at the Hôtel Crillon, his office force knew far more about the proceedings than did the three American Commissioners who were not present. As the House organization made no effort to hide the fact that they had inside information, the representatives of the press as a consequence frequented the office of the Colonel in search of the latest news concerning the Commission on the League of Nations.

But, in addition to the embarrassment caused the American Commissioners and the unenviable position in which they were placed by the secrecy with which the President surrounded his intercourse with the foreign statesmen and the proceedings of the Commission on the League of Nations, his secret negotiations caused the majority of the delegates to the Conference and the public at large to lose in a large measure their confidence in the actuality of his devotion to "open diplomacy," which he had so unconditionally proclaimed in the first of his Fourteen Points. If the policy of secrecy had ceased with the discussions preliminary to the organization of the Conference, or even with those preceding the meetings of the Commission on the League of Nations, criticism and complaint would doubtless have ceased, but as the negotiations progressed the secrecy of the conferences of the leaders increased rather than decreased, culminating at last in the organization of the Council of Four, the most powerful and most seclusive of the councils which directed the proceedings at Paris. Behind closed doors these four individuals, who controlled the policies of the United States, Great Britain, France, and Italy, passed final judgment on the mass of articles which entered into the Treaties of Peace, but kept their decisions secret except from the committee which was drafting the articles.

The organization of the Council of Four and the mystery which enveloped its deliberations emphasized as nothing else could have done the secretiveness with which adjustments were being made and compromises were being effected. It directed attention also to the fact that the Four Great Powers had taken supreme control of settling the terms of peace, that they were primates among the assembled nations and that they intended to have their authority acknowledged. This extraordinary secrecy and arrogation of power by the Council of Four excited astonishment and complaint throughout the body of delegates to the Conference, and caused widespread criticism in the press and among the people of many countries.

A week after the Council of Ten was divided into the Council of the Heads of States, the official title of the

Council of Four, and the Council of Foreign Ministers, the official title of the Council of Five (popularly nicknamed "The Big Four" and "The Little Five"), I made the following note on the subject of secret negotiations:

"After the experience of the last three months [January–March, 1919] I am convinced that the method of personal interviews and private conclaves is a failure. It has given every opportunity for intrigue, plotting, bargaining, and combining. The President, as I now see it, should have insisted on everything being brought before the Plenary Conference. He would then have had the confidence and support of all the smaller nations because they would have looked up to him as their champion and guide. They would have followed him.

"The result of the present method has been to destroy their faith and arouse their resentment. They look upon the President as in favor of a world ruled by Five Great Powers, an international despotism of the strong, in which the little nations are merely rubber-stamps.

"The President has undoubtedly found himself in a most difficult position. He has put himself on a level with politicians experienced in intrigue, whom he will find a pretty difficult lot. He will sink in the estimation of the delegates who are not within the inner circle, and what will be still more disastrous will be the loss of confidence among the peoples of the nations represented here. A grievous blunder has been made."

The views, which I expressed in this note in regard to the unwisdom of the President's course, were not new at the time that I wrote them. Over two months before I had watched the practice of secret negotiation with apprehension as to what the effect would be upon the President's influence and standing with the delegates to the Conference. I then believed that he was taking a dangerous course which he would in the end regret. So strong was this conviction that during a meeting, which the President held with the American Commissioners on the evening of January 29, I told him bluntly — perhaps too bluntly from the point of view of policy — that I considered the secret interviews which he was holding with the European statesmen, where no witnesses were present, were unwise, that he was far more successful in accomplishment and less liable to be misunderstood if he confined his negotiating to the Council of Ten, and that, furthermore, acting through the Council he would be much less subject to public criticism. I supported these views with the statement that the general secrecy, which was being practiced, was making a very bad impression everywhere, and for that reason, if for no other, I was opposed to it. The silence with which the President received my remarks appeared to me significant of his attitude toward this advice, and his subsequent continuance of secret methods without change, unless it was to increase the secrecy, proved that our judgments were not in accord on the subject. The only result of my representations, it would seem, was to cause Mr. Wilson to realize that I was not in sympathy with his way of conducting the negotiations. In the circumstances I think now that it was a blunder on my part to have stated my views so frankly.

Two days after I wrote the note, which is quoted (April 2, 1919), I made another note more general in character, but in which appears the following:

"Everywhere there are developing bitterness and resentment against a secretiveness which is interpreted to mean failure. The patience of the people is worn threadbare. Their temper has grown ragged. They are sick of whispering diplomats.

"Muttered confidences, secret intrigues, and the tactics of the 'gum-shoer' are discredited. The world wants none of them these days. It despises and loathes them. What the world asks are honest declarations openly proclaimed. The statesman who seeks to gain his end by tortuous and underground ways is foolish or badly advised. The public man who is sly and secretive rather than frank and bold, whose methods are devious rather than obvious, pursues a dangerous path which leads neither to glory nor to success.

"Secret diplomacy, the bane of the past, is a menace from which man believed himself to be rid. He who resurrects it invites condemnation. The whole world will rejoice when the day of the whisperer is over."

This note, read at the present time, sounds extravagant in thought and intemperate in expression. It was written under the influence of emotions which had been deeply stirred by the conditions then existing. Time usually softens one's judgments and the passage of events makes less vivid one's impressions. The perspective, however, grows clearer and the proportions more accurate when the observer stands at a distance. While the language of the note might well be changed and made less florid, the thought needs little modification. The public criticism was widespread and outspoken, and from the expressions used it was very evident that there prevailed a general popular disapproval of the way the negotiations were being conducted. The Council of Four won the press-name of "The Olympians," and much was said of "the thick cloud of mystery" which hid them from the anxious multitudes, and of the secrecy which veiled their deliberations. The newspapers and the correspondents at Paris openly complained and the delegates to the Conference in a more guarded way showed their bitterness at the overlordship assumed by the leading statesmen of the Great Powers and the secretive methods which they employed. It was, as may be gathered from the note quoted, a distressing and depressing time.

As concrete examples of the evils of secret negotiations the "Fiume Affair" and the "Shantung Settlement" are the best known because of the storm of criticism and protest which they caused. As the Shantung Settlement was one of the chief matters of difference between the President and myself, it will be treated later. The case of Fiume is different. As to the merits of the question I was very much in accord with the President, but to the bungling way in which it was handled I was strongly opposed believing that secret interviews, at which false hopes were encouraged, were at the bottom of all the trouble which later developed. But for this secrecy I firmly believe that there would have been no "Fiume Affair."

The discussion of the Italian claims to territory along the northern boundary of the Kingdom and about the head of the Adriatic Sea began as soon as the American Commission was installed at Paris, about the middle of December, 1918. The endeavor of the Italian emissaries was to induce the Americans, particularly the President, to recognize the boundary laid down in the Pact of London. That agreement, which Italy had required Great Britain and France to accept in April, 1915, before she consented to declare war against the Austro-Hungarian Empire, committed the Entente Powers to the recognition of Italy's right to certain territorial acquisitions at the expense of Austria-Hungary in the event of the defeat of the Central Empires. By the boundary line agreed upon in the Pact, Italy would obtain certain important islands and ports on the Dalmatian coast in addition to the Austrian Tyrol and the Italian provinces of the Dual Monarchy at the head of the Adriatic.

When this agreement was signed, the dissolution of Austria-Hungary was not in contemplation, or at least, if it was considered, the possibility of its accomplishment seemed very remote. It was assumed that the Dalmatian territory to be acquired under the treaty to be negotiated in accordance with the terms of the Pact would, with the return of the Italian provinces, give to Italy naval control over the Adriatic Sea and secure the harborless eastern coast of the Italian peninsula against future hostile attack by the Austro-Hungarian Empire. The boundary laid

down in the agreement was essentially strategic and based
primarily on considerations of Italian national safety. As
long as the Empire existed as a Great Power the boundary
of the Pact of London, so far as it related to the Adriatic
littoral and islands, was not unreasonable or the territorial
demands excessive.

But the close of active warfare in the autumn of 1918,
when the armistice went into effect, found conditions
wholly different from those upon which these territorial
demands had been predicated. The Austro-Hungarian
Empire had fallen to pieces beyond the hope of becoming
again one of the Great Powers. The various nationalities,
which had long been restless and unhappy under the rule
of the Hapsburgs, threw off the imperial yoke, proclaimed
their independence, and sought the recognition and protection of the Allies. The Poles of the Empire joined their
brethren of the Polish provinces of Russia and Prussia in
the resurrection of their ancient nation; Bohemia, Moravia, and Slovakia united in forming the new state of
Czecho-Slovakia; the southern Slavs of Croatia, Slavonia,
Bosnia, Herzegovina, and Dalmatia announced their union
with their kindred of the Kingdom of Serbia; and Hungary declared the severance of her political union with
Austria. In a word the Dual Empire ceased to exist. It
was no longer a menace to the national safety of Italy.
This was the state of affairs when the delegates to the
Peace Conference began to assemble at Paris.

The Italian statesmen realized that these new conditions

might raise serious questions as to certain territorial cessions which would come to Italy under the terms of the
Pact of London, because their strategic necessity had disappeared with the dissolution of Austria-Hungary. While
they had every reason to assume that Great Britain and
France would live up to their agreement, it was hardly to
be expected that under the changed conditions and in the
circumstances attending the negotiation and signature of
the Pact, the British and French statesmen would be disposed to protest against modifications of the proposed
boundary if the United States and other nations, not parties to the agreement, should insist upon changes as a matter of justice to the new state of the Serbs, Croats, and
Slovenes. It apparently was considered expedient, by the
Italian representatives, in view of the situation which had
developed, to increase rather than to reduce their claims
along the Dalmatian coast in order that they might have
something which could be surrendered in a compromise
without giving up the boundaries laid down in the Pact
of London.

It is probable, too, that these additional claims were advanced by Italy in order to offset in a measure the claims
of the Jugo-Slavs, who through the Serbian delegates at
Paris were making territorial demands which the Italians
declared to be extravagant and which, if granted, would
materially reduce the proposed cessions to Italy under the
Pact of London. Furthermore, the Italian Government
appeared to be by no means pleased with the idea of a

Jugo-Slav state so strong that it might become a commercial, if not a naval, rival of Italy in the Adriatic. The Italian delegates in private interviews showed great bitterness toward the Slavs, who, they declared, had, as Austrian subjects, waged war against Italy and taken part in the cruel and wanton acts attendant upon the invasion of the northern Italian provinces. They asserted that it was unjust to permit these people, by merely changing their allegiance after defeat, to escape punishment for the outrages which they had committed against Italians and actually to profit by being vanquished. This antipathy to the Slavs of the former Empire was in a measure transferred to the Serbs, who were naturally sympathetic with their kinsmen and who were also ambitious to build up a strong Slav state with a large territory and with commercial facilities on the Adriatic coast which would be ample to meet the trade needs of the interior.

While there may have been a certain fear for the national safety of Italy in having as a neighbor a Slav state with a large and virile population, extensive resources, and opportunity to become a naval power in the Mediterranean, the real cause of apprehension seemed to be that the new nation would become a commercial rival of Italy in the Adriatic and prevent her from securing the exclusive control of the trade which her people coveted and which the complete victory over Austria-Hungary appeared to assure to them.

The two principal ports having extensive facilities for

shipping and rail-transportation to and from the Danu-
bian provinces of the Dual Empire were Trieste and Fiume.
The other Dalmatian ports were small and without possibilities of extensive development, while the precipitous
mountain barrier between the coast and the interior which
rose almost from the water-line rendered railway construction from an engineering standpoint impracticable if
not impossible. It was apparent that, if Italy could obtain
both the port of Trieste and the port of Fiume, the two
available outlets for foreign trade to the territories lying
north and east of the Adriatic Sea, she would have a substantial monopoly of the sea-borne commerce of the Dalmatian coast and its hinterland. It was equally apparent
that Italian possession of the two ports would place the
new Slav state at a great disadvantage commercially, as
the principal volume of its exports and imports would have
to pass through a port in the hands of a trade rival which
could, in case of controversy or in order to check competi-
tion, be closed to Slav ships and goods on this or that pre-
text, even if the new state found it practicable to maintain
a merchant marine under an agreement granting it the use
of the port.

In view of the new conditions which had thus arisen
through the dissolution of the Austro-Hungarian Empire
and the union of the Southern Slavs, the Italian delegates
at Paris began a vigorous campaign to obtain sovereignty,
or at least administrative control, over Fiume and the
adjacent coasts and islands, it having been generally con-

ceded that Trieste should be ceded to Italy. The Italian demand for Fiume had become real instead of artificial. This campaign was conducted by means of personal interviews with the representatives of the principal Powers, and particularly with those of the United States because it was apparently felt that the chief opposition to the demand would come from that quarter, since the President was known to favor the general proposition that every nation should have free access to the sea and, if possible, a seaport under its own sovereignty.

The Italian delegates were undoubtedly encouraged by some Americans to believe that, while the President had not actually declared in favor of Italian control of Fiume, he was sympathetic to the idea and would ultimately assent to it just as he had in the case of the cession to Italy of the Tyrol with its Austrian population. Convinced by these assurances of success the Italian leaders began a nation-wide propaganda at home for the purpose of arousing a strong public sentiment for the acquisition of the port. This propaganda was begun, it would seem, for two reasons, first, the political advantage to be gained when it was announced that Signor Orlando and his colleagues at Paris had succeeded in having their demand recognized, and, second, the possibility of influencing the President to a speedy decision by exhibiting the intensity and unity of the Italian national spirit in demanding the annexation of the little city, the major part of the population of which was asserted to be of Italian blood.

The idea, which was industriously circulated throughout Italy, that Fiume was an Italian city, aroused the feelings of the people more than any political or economic argument could have done. The fact that the suburbs, which were really as much a part of the municipality as the area within the city proper, were inhabited largely by Jugo-Slavs was ignored, ridiculed, or denied. That the Jugo-Slavs undoubtedly exceeded in numbers the Italians in the community when it was treated as a whole made no difference to the propagandists who asserted that Fiume was Italian. They clamored for its annexation on the ground of "self-determination," though refusing to accept that principle as applicable to the inhabitants of the Austrian Tyrol and failing to raise any question in regard to it in the case of the port of Danzig. The Italian orators and press were not disturbed by the inconsistency of their positions, and the Italian statesmen at Paris, when their attention was called to it, replied that the cases were not the same, an assertion which it would have been difficult to establish with facts or support with convincing arguments.

While the propaganda went forward in Italy with increasing energy, additional assurances, I was informed by one of the Italian group, were given to Signor Orlando and Baron Sonnino that President Wilson was almost on the point of conceding the justice of the Italian claim to Fiume. It was not until the latter part of March, 1919, that these statesmen began to suspect that they had been misinformed and that the influence of their American friends was not as powerful with Mr. Wilson as they had been led to believe. It was an unpleasant awakening. They were placed in a difficult position. Too late to calm the inflamed temper of the Italian people the Italian leaders at Paris had no alternative but to press their demands with greater vigor since the failure to obtain Fiume meant almost inevitable disaster to the Orlando Ministry.

Following conversations with Baron Sonnino and some others connected with the Italian delegation, I drew the conclusion that they would go so far as to refuse to make peace with Germany unless the Adriatic Question was first settled to their satisfaction. In a memorandum dated March 29, I wrote: "This will cause a dangerous crisis," and in commenting on the probable future of the subject I stated:

"My fear is that the President will continue to rely upon private interviews and his powers of persuasion to induce the Italians to abandon their extravagant claim. I am sure that he will not be able to do it. On the contrary, his conversations will strengthen rather than weaken Italian determination. He ought to tell them *now* that he will not consent to have Fiume given to Italy. It would cause anger and bitterness, but nothing to compare with the resentment which will be aroused if the uncertainty is permitted to go on much longer. I shall tell the President my opinion at the first opportunity. [I did this a few days later.]

"The future is darkened by the Adriatic situation and I look to an explosion before the matter is settled. It is a good thing that the President visited Italy when he did and when blessings rather than curses greeted him. Secret diplomacy is reaping a new harvest of execrations and condemnations. Will the practice ever cease?"

During the first three weeks of April the efforts to shake the determination of the President to support the Jugo-Slav claims to Fiume and the adjacent territory were redoubled, but without avail. Every form of compromise as to boundary and port privileges, which did not deprive Italy of the sovereignty, was proposed, but found to be unacceptable. The Italians, held by the pressure of the aroused national spirit, and the President, firm in the conviction that the Italian claim to the port was unjust, remained obdurate. Attempts were made by both sides to reach some common ground for an agreement, but none was found. As the time approached to submit the Treaty to the German plenipotentiaries, who were expected to arrive at Paris on April 26, the Italian delegates let it be known that they would absent themselves from the meeting at which the document was to be presented unless a satisfactory understanding in regard to Fiume was obtained before the meeting. I doubt whether this threat was with the approval and upon the advice of the American friends of the Italians who had been industrious in attempting to persuade the President to accept a compromise. An American familiar with Mr. Wilson's disposition would have realized that to try to coerce him in that manner would be folly, as in all probability it would have just the contrary effect to the one desired.

The Italian delegates did not apparently read the President's temper aright. They made a mistake. Their threat of withdrawal from the Conference resulted far differently from their expectation and hope. When Mr. Wilson learned of the Italian threat he met it with a public announcement of his position in regard to the controversy, which was intended as an appeal to the people of Italy to abandon the claim to Fiume and to reject their Government's policy of insisting on an unjust settlement. This declaration was given to the press late in the afternoon of April 23, and a French newspaper containing it was handed, it was said, to Signor Orlando at the President's residence where the Council of Four were assembled. He immediately withdrew, issued a counter-statement, and the following day left Paris for Rome more on account of his indignation at the course taken by the President than because of the threat which he had made. Baron Sonnino also departed the next day.

It is not my purpose to pursue further the course of events following the crisis which was precipitated by the President's published statement and the resulting departure of the principal Italian delegates. The effect on the Italian people is common knowledge. A tempest of popular fury against the President swept over Italy from end to end. From being the most revered of all men by the Italians, he became the most detested. As no words of praise and admiration were too extravagant to be spoken of him when he visited Rome in January, so no words of insult or

execration were too gross to characterize him after his public announcement regarding the Adriatic Question. There
was never a more complete reversal of public sentiment
toward an individual.

The reason for reciting the facts of the Fiume dispute,
which was one of the most unpleasant incidents that took
place at Paris during the negotiations, is to bring out
clearly the consequences of secret diplomacy. A discussion
of the reasons, or of the probable reasons, for the return
of the Italian statesmen to Paris before the Treaty was
handed to the Germans would add nothing to the subject
under consideration, while the same may be said of the
subsequent occupation of Fiume by Italian nationalists
under the fanatical D'Annunzio, without authority of
their Government, but with the enthusiastic approval of
the Italian people.

Five days after the Italian Premier and his Minister of
Foreign Affairs had departed from Paris I had a long interview with a well-known Italian diplomat, who was an intimate friend of both Signor Orlando and Baron Sonnino
and who had been very active in the secret negotiations
regarding the Italian boundaries which had been taking
place at Paris since the middle of December. This diplomat was extremely bitter about the whole affair and took
no pains to hide his views as to the causes of the critical
situation which existed. In the memorandum of our conversation, which I wrote immediately after he left my
office, appears the following:

"He exclaimed: 'One tells you one thing and that is not true; then another tells you another thing and that too is not true. What is one to believe? What can one do? It is hopeless. So many secret meetings with different persons are simply awful' — He threw up his hands — 'Now we have the result. It is terrible!'

"I laughed and said, 'I conclude that you do not like secret diplomacy.'

" 'I do not; I do not,' he fervently exclaimed. 'All our trouble comes from these secret meetings of four men [referring to the Big Four], who keep no records and who tell different stories of what takes place. Secrecy is to blame. We have been unable to rely on any one. To have to run around and see this man and that man is not the way to do. Most all sympathize with you when alone and then they desert you when they get with others. This is the cause of much bitterness and distrust. *Secret diplomacy is an utter failure*. It is too hard to endure. Some men know only how to whisper. They are not to be trusted. I do not like it.'

" 'Well,' I said, 'you cannot charge me with that way of doing business.'

" 'I cannot,' he replied, 'you tell me the truth. I may not like it, but at least you do not hold out false hopes.' "

The foregoing conversation no doubt expressed the real sentiments of the members of the Italian delegation at that time. Disgust with confidential personal interviews and with relying upon personal influence rather than upon the merits of their case was the natural reaction following the failure to win by these means the President's approval of Italy's demands.

The Italian policy in relation to Fiume was wrecked on

the rock of President Wilson's firm determination that the Jugo-Slavs should have a seaport on the Adriatic sufficient for their needs and that Italy should not control the approaches to that port. With the wreck of the Fiume policy went in time the Orlando Government which had failed to make good the promises which they had given to their people. Too late they realized that secret diplomacy had failed, and that they had made a mistake in relying upon it. It is no wonder that the two leaders of the Italian delegation on returning to Paris and resuming their duties in the Conference refrained from attempting to arrange clandestinely the settlement of the Adriatic Question. The "go-betweens," on whom they had previously relied, were no longer employed. Secret diplomacy was anathema. They had paid a heavy price for the lesson, which they had learned.

When one reviews the negotiations at Paris from December, 1918, to June, 1919, the secretiveness which characterized them is very evident. Everybody seemed to talk in whispers and never to say anything worth while except in confidence. The open sessions of the Conference were arranged beforehand. They were formal and perfunctory. The agreements and bargains were made behind closed doors. This secrecy began with the exchange of views concerning the League of Nations, following which came the creation of the Council of Ten, whose meetings were intended to be secret. Then came the secret sessions of the Commission on the League and the numerous informal interviews of the President with one or more of the Premiers of the Allied Powers, the facts concerning which were not divulged to the American Commissioners. Later, on Mr. Wilson's return from the United States, dissatisfaction with and complaint of the publicity given to some of the proceedings of the Council of Ten induced the formation of the Council of Four with the result that the secrecy of the negotiations was practically unbroken. If to this brief summary of the increasing secretiveness of the proceedings of the controlling bodies of the Peace Conference are added the intrigues and personal bargainings which were constantly going on, the "log-rolling" — to use a term familiar to American politics — which was practiced, the record is one which invites no praise and will find many who condemn it.

In view of the frequent and emphatic declarations in favor of "open diplomacy" and the popular interpretation placed upon the phrase "Open covenants openly arrived at," the effect of the secretive methods employed by the leading negotiators at Paris was to destroy public confidence in the sincerity of these statesmen and to subject them to the charge of pursuing a policy which they had themselves condemned and repudiated. Naturally President Wilson, who had been especially earnest in his denunciation of secret negotiations, suffered more than his foreign colleagues, whose real support of "open diplomacy" had always been doubted, though all of them in a measure fell in public estimation as a consequence of the way in which the negotiations were conducted.

The criticism and condemnation, expressed with varying degrees of intensity, resulted from the disappointed hopes of the peoples of the world, who had looked forward confidently to the Peace Conference at Paris as the first great and decisive change to a new diplomacy which would cast aside the cloak of mystery that had been in the past the recognized livery of diplomatic negotiations. The record of the Paris proceedings in this particular is a sorry one. It is the record of the abandonment of principle, of the failure to follow precepts unconditionally proclaimed, of the repudiation by act, if not by word, of a new and better type of international intercourse.

It is not my purpose or desire to fix the blame for this perpetuation of old and discredited practices on any one individual. To do so would be unjust, since more than one preferred the old way and should share the responsibility for its continuance. But, as the secrecy became more and more impenetrable and as the President gave silent acquiescence or at least failed to show displeasure with the practice, I realized that in this matter, as in others, our judgments were at variance and our views irreconcilable. As my opposition to the method of conducting the proceedings was evident, I cannot but assume that this decided difference was one that materially affected the relations between Mr. Wilson and myself and that he looked upon me as an unfavorable critic of his course in permitting to go unprotested the secrecy which characterized the negotiations.

The attention of the delegates to the Peace Conference who represented the smaller nations was early directed to their being denied knowledge of the terms of the Treaty which were being formulated by the principal members of the delegations of the Five Great Powers. There is no doubt that at the first their mental attitude was one of confidence that the policy of secrecy would not be continued beyond the informal meetings preliminary to and necessary for arranging the organization and procedure of the Conference; but, as the days lengthened into weeks and the weeks into months, and as the information concerning the actual negotiations, which reached them, became more and more meager, they could no longer close their eyes to the fact that their national rights and aspirations were to be recognized or denied by the leaders of the Great Powers without the consent and even without the full knowledge of the delegates of the nations vitally interested.

Except in the case of a few of these delegates, who had been able to establish intimate personal relations with some of the "Big Four," the secretiveness of the discussions and decisions regarding the Treaty settlements aroused amazement and indignation. It was evident that it was to be a "dictated peace" and not a "negotiated peace," a peace dictated by the Great Powers not only to the enemy, but also to their fellow belligerents. Some of the delegates spoke openly in criticism of the furtive methods that were being employed, but the majority held their peace. It can hardly be doubted, however, that the body of delegates were practically unanimous in disapproving the secrecy of the proceedings, and this disapproval was to be found even among the delegations of the Great Powers. It was accepted by the lesser nations because it seemed impolitic and useless to oppose the united will of the controlling oligarchy. It was natural that the delegates of the less influential states should feel that their countries would suffer in the terms of peace if they openly denounced the treatment accorded them as violative of the dignity of representatives of independent sovereignties. In any event no formal protest was entered against their being deprived of a knowledge to which they were entitled, a deprivation which placed them and their countries in a subordinate, and, to an extent, a humiliating, position.

The climax of this policy of secrecy toward the body of delegates came on the eve of the delivery of the Treaty of Peace to the German representatives who were awaiting that event at Versailles. By a decision of the Council of the Heads of States, reached three weeks before the time, only a digest or summary of the Treaty was laid before the plenary session of the Conference on the Preliminaries of Peace on the day preceding the delivery of the full text of the Treaty to the Germans. The delegates of the smaller belligerent nations were not permitted to examine the actual text of the document before it was seen by their defeated adversaries. Nations, which had fought valiantly and suffered agonies during the war, were treated with no more consideration than their enemies so far as knowledge of the exact terms of peace were concerned. The arguments, which could be urged on the ground of the practical necessity of a small group dealing with the questions and determining the settlements, seem insufficient to justify the application of the rule of secrecy to the delegates who sat in the Conference on the Preliminaries of Peace. It is not too severe to say that it outraged the equal rights of independent and sovereign states and under less critical conditions would have been resented as an insult by the plenipotentiaries of the lesser nations. Even within the delegations of the Great Powers there were indignant murmurings against this indefensible and unheard-of treatment of allies. No man, whose mind was not warped by prejudice or dominated by political expediency, could give it his approval or become its apologist. Secrecy, and intrigues which were only possible through secrecy, stained nearly all the negotiations at Paris, but in this final act of withholding knowledge of the actual text of the Treaty from the delegates of most of the nations represented in the Conference the spirit of secretiveness seems to have gone mad.

The psychological effects of secrecy on those who are kept in ignorance are not difficult to analyze. They follow normal processes and may be thus stated: Secrecy breeds suspicion; suspicion, doubt; doubt, distrust; and distrust produces lack of frankness, which is closely akin to secrecy. The result is a vicious circle, of which deceit and intrigue are the very essence. Secrecy and its natural consequences have given to diplomacy a popular reputation for trickery, for double-dealing, and in a more or less degree for unscrupulous and dishonest methods of obtaining desired ends, a reputation that has found expression in the ironic definition of a diplomat as "an honest man sent to lie abroad for the good of his country."

The time had arrived when the bad name which diplomacy had so long borne could and should have been removed. "Open covenants openly arrived at" appealed to the popular feeling of antipathy toward secret diplomacy, of which the Great War was generally believed to be the product. The Paris Conference appeared to offer an inviting opportunity to turn the page and to begin a new and better chapter in the annals of international intercourse. To do this required a fixed purpose to abandon the old methods, to insist on openness and candor, to refuse to be drawn into whispered agreements. The choice between the old and the new ways had to be definite and final. It had to be made at the very beginning of the negotiations. It was made. Secrecy was adopted. Thus diplomacy, in spite of the announced intention to reform its practices, has retained the evil taint which makes it out of harmony with the spirit of good faith and of open dealing which is characteristic of the best thought of the present epoch. There is little to show that diplomacy has been raised to a higher plane or has won a better reputation in the world at large than it possessed before the nations assembled at

Paris to make peace. This failure to lift the necessary agency of international relations out of the rut worn deep by centuries of practice is one of the deplorable consequences of the peace negotiations. So much might have been done; nothing was done.

CHAPTER XVIII
THE SHANTUNG SETTLEMENT

THE Shantung Settlement was not so evidently chargeable to secret negotiations as the crisis over the disposition of Fiume, but the decision was finally reached through that method. The controversy between Japan and China as to which country should become the possessor of the former German property and rights in the Shantung Peninsula was not decided until almost the last moment before the Treaty with Germany was completed. Under pressure of the necessity of making the document ready for delivery to the German delegates, President Wilson, M. Clemenceau, and Mr. Lloyd George, composing the Council of the Heads of States in the absence of Signor Orlando in Rome, issued an order directing the Drafting Committee of the Conference to prepare articles for the Treaty embodying the decision that the Council had made. This decision, which was favorable to the Japanese claims, was the result of a confidential arrangement with the Japanese delegates by which, in the event of their claims being granted, they withdrew their threat to decline to sign the Treaty of Peace, agreed not to insist on a proposed amendment to the Covenant declaring for racial equality, and orally promised to restore to China in the near future certain rights of sovereignty over the territory, which promise failed of confirmation in writing or by formal public declaration.

It is fair to presume that, if the conflicting claims of Japan and China to the alleged rights of Germany in Chinese territory had been settled upon the merits through the medium of an impartial commission named by the Conference, the Treaty provisions relating to the disposition of those rights would have been very different from those which "The Three" ordered to be drafted. Before a commission of the Conference no persuasive reasons for conceding the Japanese claims could have been urged on the basis of an agreement on the part of Japan to adhere to the League of Nations or to abandon the attempt to have included in the Covenant a declaration of equality between races. It was only through secret interviews and secret agreements that the threat of the Japanese delegates could be successfully made. An adjustment on such a basis had nothing to do with the justice of the case or with the legal rights and principles involved. The threat was intended to coerce the arbiters of the treaty terms by menacing the success of the plan to establish a League of Nations — to use an ugly word, it was a species of "blackmail" not unknown to international relations in the past. It was made possible because the sessions of the Council of the Heads of States and the conversations concerning Shantung were secret.

It was a calamity for the Republic of China and unfortunate for the presumed justice written into the Treaty that President Wilson was convinced that the Japanese delegates would decline to accept the Covenant of the League of Nations if the claims of Japan to the German rights were denied. It was equally unfortunate that the President felt that without Japan's adherence to the Covenant the formation of the League would be endangered if not actually prevented. And it was especially unfortunate that the President considered the formation of the League in accordance with the provisions of the Covenant to be superior to every other consideration and that to accomplish this object almost any sacrifice would be justifiable.

It is my impression that the departure of Signor Orlando and Baron Sonnino from Paris and the uncertainty of their return to give formal assent to the Treaty with Germany, an uncertainty which existed at the time of the decision of the Shantung Question, had much to do with the anxiety of the President as to Japan's attitude. He doubtless felt that to have two of the Five Great Powers decline at the last moment to accept the Treaty containing the Covenant would jeopardize the plan for a League and would greatly encourage his opponents in the United States. His line of reasoning was logical, but in my judgment was based on the false premise that the Japanese would carry out their threat to refuse to accept the Treaty and enter the League of Nations unless they obtained a cession of the German rights. I did not believe at the time, and I do not believe now, that Japan would have made good her threat. The superior international position, which she held as one of the Five Great Powers in the Conference, and which she would hold in the League of Nations as one of the Principal Powers in the constitution of the Executive Council, would never have been abandoned by the Tokio Government. The Japanese delegates would not have run the risk of losing this position by adopting the course pursued by the Italians.

The cases were different. No matter what action was taken by Italy she would have continued to be a Great Power in any organization of the world based on a classification of the nations. If she did not enter the League under the German Treaty, she certainly would later and would undoubtedly hold an influential position in the organization whether her delegates signed the Covenant or accepted it in another treaty or by adherence. It was not so with Japan. There were reasons to believe that, if she failed to become one of the Principal Powers at the outset, another opportunity might never be given her to obtain so high a place in the concert of the nations. The seats that her delegates had in the Council of Ten had caused criticism and dissatisfaction in certain quarters, and the elimination of a Japanese from the Council of the Heads of States showed that the Japanese position as an equal of the other Great Powers was by no means secure. These indications of Japan's place in the international oligarchy must have been evident to her plenipotentiaries at Paris, who in all probability reported the situation to Tokio. From the point of view of policy the execution of the threat of withdrawal presented dangers to Japan's prestige which the diplomats who represented her would never have incurred if they were as cautious and shrewd as they appeared to be. The President did not hold this opinion. We differed radically in our judgment as to the sincerity of the Japanese threat. He showed that he believed it would be carried out. I believed that it would not be.

It has not come to my knowledge what the attitude of the British and French statesmen was concerning the disposition of the Shantung rights, although I have read the views of certain authors on the subject, but I do know that the actual decision lay with the President. If he had declined to recognize the Japanese claims, they would never have been granted nor would the grant have been written into the Treaty. Everything goes to show that he realized this responsibility and that the cession to Japan was not made through error or misconception of the rights of the parties, but was done deliberately and with a full appreciation that China was being denied that which in other circumstances would have been awarded to her. If it had not been for reasons wholly independent and outside of the question in dispute, the President would not have decided as he did.

It is not my purpose to enter into the details of the origin of the German lease of Kiao-Chau (the port of Tsingtau) and of the economic concessions in the Province of Shantung acquired by Germany. Suffice it to say that, taking advantage of a situation caused by the murder of some missionary priests in the province, the German Government in 1898 forced the Chinese Government to make treaties granting for the period of ninety-nine years the lease and concessions, by which the sovereign authority over this "Holy Land" of China was to all intents ceded to Germany, which at once improved the harbor, fortified the leased area, and began railway construction and the exploitation of the Shantung Peninsula.

The outbreak of the World War found Germany in possession of the leased area and in substantial control of the territory under the concession. On August 15, 1914, the Japanese Government presented an *ultimatum* to the German Government, in which the latter was required "to deliver on a date not later than September 15 to the Imperial Japanese authorities, without condition or compensation, the entire leased territory of Kiao-Chau with a view to the eventual restoration of the same to China."

On the German failure to comply with these demands the Japanese Government landed troops and, in company with a small British contingent, took possession of the leased port and occupied the territory traversed by the German railway, even to the extent of establishing a civil government in addition to garrisoning the line with Japanese troops. Apparently the actual occupation of this Chinese territory induced a change in the policy of the Imperial Government at Tokio, for in December, 1914, Baron Kato, the Minister of Foreign Affairs, declared that the restoration of Tsingtau to China "is to be settled in

the future" and that the Japanese Government had made
no promises to do so.

This statement, which seemed in contradiction of the
ultimatum to Germany, was made in the Japanese Diet. It
was followed up in January, 1915, by the famous "Twenty-
one Demands" made upon the Government at Peking. It
is needless to go into these demands further than to quote
the first to which China was to subscribe.

"The Chinese Government agrees that when the Japanese Government hereafter approaches the German Government for the transfer of all rights and privileges of
whatsoever nature enjoyed by Germany in the Province
of Shantung, whether secured by treaty or in any other
manner, China shall give her full assent thereto."

The important point to be noted in this demand is that
Japan did not consider that the occupation of Kiao-Chau
and the seizure of the German concessions transferred title
to her, but looked forward to a future transfer by treaty.

The "Twenty-one Demands" were urged with persistency by the Japanese Government and finally took the
form of an *ultimatum* as to all but Group V of the "Demands." The Peking Government was in no political or
military condition to resist, and, in order to avoid an open
rupture with their aggressive neighbor, entered into a
treaty granting the Japanese demands.

China, following the action which the United States had
taken on February 3, 1917, severed diplomatic relations
with Germany on March 14, and five months later de-

clared war against her announcing at the same time that the treaties, conventions, and agreements between the two countries were by the declaration abrogated. As to whether a state of war does in fact abrogate a treaty of the character of the Sino-German Treaty of 1898 some question may be raised under the accepted rules of international law, on the ground that it was a cession of sovereign rights and constituted an international servitude in favor of Germany over the territory affected by it. But in this particular case the indefensible duress employed by the German Government to compel China to enter into the treaty introduces another factor into the problem and excepts it from any general rule that treaties of that nature are merely suspended and not abrogated by war between the parties. It would seem as if no valid argument could be made in favor of suspension because the effect of the rule would be to revive and perpetuate an inequitable and unjustifiable act. Morally and legally the Chinese Government was right in denouncing the treaty and agreements with Germany and in treating the territorial rights acquired by coercion as extinguished.

It would appear, therefore, that, as the Japanese Government recognized that the rights in the Province of Shantung had not passed to Japan by the forcible occupation of Kiao-Chau and the German concessions, those rights ceased to exist when China declared war against Germany, and that China was, therefore, entitled to resume full sovereignty over the area where such rights previously existed.

It is true that subsequently, on September 24, 1918, the Chinese and Japanese Governments by exchange of notes at Tokio entered into agreements affecting the Japanese occupation of the Kiao-Chau–Tsinan Railway and the adjoining territory, but the governmental situation at Peking was too precarious to refuse any demands made by the Japanese Government. In fact the action of the Japanese Government was very similar to that of the German Government in 1898. An examination of these notes discloses the fact that the Japanese were in possession of the denounced German rights, but nothing in the notes indicates that they were there as a matter of legal right, or that the Chinese Government conceded their right of occupation.

This was the state of affairs when the Peace Conference assembled at Paris. Germany had by force compelled China in 1898 to cede to her certain rights in the Province of Shantung. Japan had seized these rights by force in 1914 and had by threats forced China in 1915 to agree to accept her disposition of them when they were legally transferred by treaty at the end of the war. China in 1917 had, on entering the war against Germany, denounced all treaties and agreements with Germany, so that the ceded rights no longer existed and could not legally be transferred by Germany to Japan by the Treaty of Peace, since the title was in China. In fact any transfer or disposition of the rights in Shantung formerly belonging to Germany was a transfer or disposition of rights belonging wholly to

China and would deprive that country of a portion of its full sovereignty over the territory affected.

While this view of the extinguishment of the German rights in Shantung was manifestly the just one and its adoption would make for the preservation of permanent peace in the Far East, the Governments of the Allied Powers had, early in 1917, and prior to the severance of diplomatic relations between China and Germany, acceded to the request of Japan to support, "on the occasion of the Peace Conference," her claims in regard to these rights which then existed. The representatives of Great Britain, France, and Italy at Paris were thus restricted, or at least embarrassed, by the promises which their Governments had made at a time when they were in no position to refuse Japan's request. They might have stood on the legal ground that the Treaty of 1898 having been abrogated by China no German rights in Shantung were in being at the time of the Peace Conference, but they apparently were unwilling to take that position. Possibly they assumed that the ground was one which they could not take in view of the undertakings of their Governments; or possibly they preferred to let the United States bear the brunt of Japanese resentment for interfering with the ambitious schemes of the Japanese Government in regard to China. There can be little doubt that political, and possibly commercial, interests influenced the attitude of the European Powers in regard to the Shantung Question.

President Wilson and the American Commissioners,

unhampered by previous commitments, were strongly opposed to acceding to the demands of the Japanese Government. The subject had been frequently considered during the early days of the negotiations and there seemed to be no divergence of views as to the justice of the Chinese claim of right to the resumption of full sovereignty over the territory affected by the lease and the concessions to Germany. These views were further strengthened by the presentation of the question before the Council of Ten. On January 27 the Japanese argued their case before the Council, the Chinese delegates being present; and on the 28th Dr. V. K. Wellington Koo spoke on behalf of China. In a note on the meeting I recorded that "he simply overwhelmed the Japanese with his argument." I believe that that opinion was common to all those who heard the two presentations. In fact it made such an impression on the Japanese themselves, that one of the delegates called upon me the following day and attempted to offset the effect by declaring that the United States, since it had not promised to support Japan's contention, would be blamed if Kiao-Chau was returned directly to China. He added that there was intense feeling in Japan in regard to the matter. It was an indirect threat of what would happen to the friendly relations between the two countries if Japan's claim was denied.

The sessions of the Commission on the League of Nations and the absence of President Wilson from Paris interrupted further consideration of the Shantung Question until the latter part of March, when the Council of Four came into being. As the subject had been fully debated in January before the Council of Ten, final decision lay with the Council of Four. What discussions took place in the latter council I do not know on account of the secrecy which was observed as to their deliberations. But I presume that the President stood firmly for the Chinese rights, as the matter remained undecided until the latter part of April.

On the 21st of April Baron Makino and Viscount Chinda called upon me in regard to the question, and I frankly told them that they ought to prove the justice of the Japanese claim, that they had not done it and that I doubted their ability to do so. I found, too, that the President had proposed that the Five Powers act as trustees of the former German rights in Shantung, but that the Japanese delegates had declared that they could not consent to the proposition, which was in the nature of a compromise intended to bridge over the existing situation that, on account of the near approach of the completion of the Treaty, was becoming more and more acute.

On April 26 the President, at a conference with the American Commissioners, showed deep concern over the existing state of the controversy, and asked me to see the Japanese delegates again and endeavor to dissuade them from insisting on their demands and to induce them to consider the international trusteeship proposed. The evening of the same day the two Japanese came by request to my office and conferred with Professor E. T. Williams, the

Commission's principal adviser on Far Eastern affairs, and with me. After an hour's conversation Viscount Chinda made it very clear that Japan intended to insist on her "pound of flesh." It was apparent both to Mr. Williams and to me that nothing could be done to obtain even a compromise, though it was on the face favorable to Japan, since it recognized the existence of the German rights, which China claimed were annulled.

On April 28 I gave a full report of the interview to Mr. White and General Bliss at our regular morning meeting. Later in the morning the President telephoned me and I informed him of the fixed determination of the Japanese to insist upon their claims. What occurred between the time of my conversation with the President and the plenary session of the Conference on the Preliminaries of Peace in the afternoon, at which the Covenant of the League of Nations was adopted, I do not actually know, but the presumption is that the Japanese were promised a satisfactory settlement in regard to Shantung, since they announced that they would not press an amendment on "racial equality" at the session, an amendment upon which they had indicated they intended to insist.

After the meeting of the Conference I made the following memorandum of the situation:

"At the Plenary Session of the Peace Conference this afternoon Baron Makino spoke of his proposed amendment to the Covenant declaring 'racial equality,' but said he would not press it.

"I concluded from what the President said to me that he was disposed to accede to Japan's claims in regard to Kiao-Chau and Shantung. He also showed me a letter from —— to Makino saying he was sorry their claims had not been finally settled before the Session.

"From all this I am forced to the conclusion that a bargain has been struck by which the Japanese agree to sign the Covenant in exchange for admission of their claims. If so, it is an iniquitous agreement.

"Apparently the President is going to do this to avoid Japan's declining to enter the League of Nations. It is a surrender of the principle of self-determination, a transfer of millions of Chinese from one foreign master to another. This is another of those secret arrangements which have riddled the 'Fourteen Points' and are wrecking a just peace.

"In my opinion it would be better to let Japan stay out of the League than to abandon China and surrender our prestige in the Far East for 'a mess of pottage' — and a mess it is. I fear that it is too late to do anything to save the situation."

Mr. White, General Bliss, and I, at our meeting that morning before the plenary session, and later when we conferred as to what had taken place at the session, were unanimous in our opinions that China's rights should be sustained even if Japan withdrew from the Peace Conference. We were all indignant at the idea of submitting to the Japanese demands and agreed that the President should be told of our attitude, because we were unwilling to have it appear that we in any way approved of acceding to Japan's claims or even of compromising them.

THE DAILY CONFERENCE OF THE AMERICAN PEACE COMMISSION

General Bliss volunteered to write the President a letter on the subject, a course which Mr. White and I heartily endorsed.

The next morning the General read the following letter to us and with our entire approval sent it to Mr. Wilson:

"Hôtel de Crillon, Paris
"April 29, 1919

"MY DEAR MR. PRESIDENT:

"Last Saturday morning you told the American Delegation that you desired suggestions, although not at that moment, in regard to the pending matter of certain conflicting claims between Japan and China centering about the alleged German rights. My principal interest in the matter is with sole reference to the question of the moral right or wrong involved. From this point of view I discussed the matter this morning with Mr. Lansing and Mr. White. They concurred with me and requested me to draft a hasty note to you on the subject.

"Since your conference with us last Saturday, I have asked myself three or four Socratic questions the answers to which make me, personally, quite sure on which side the moral right lies.

"*First.* Japan bases certain of her claims on the right acquired by conquest. I asked myself the following questions: Suppose Japan had not succeeded in her efforts to force the capitulation of the Germans at Tsing-Tsau; suppose that the armistice of November 11th had found her still fighting the Germans at that place, just as the armistice found the English still fighting the Germans in South-East Africa. We would then oblige Germany to dispose of her claims in China by a clause in the Treaty of Peace. Would it occur to any one that, as a matter of right, we should force Germany to cede her claims to Japan rather than to China? It seems to me that it would occur to every American that we would then have the opportunity that we have long desired to force Germany to correct, in favor of China, the great wrong which she began to do to the latter in 1898. What moral right has Japan acquired by her conquest of Shantung assisted by the British? If Great Britain and Japan secured no moral right to sovereignty over various savages inhabiting islands in the Pacific Ocean, but, on the other hand, we held that these peoples shall be governed by mandates under the League of Nations, what moral right has Japan acquired to the suzerainty (which she would undoubtedly eventually have) over 30,000,000 Chinese in the sacred province of Shantung?

"*Second.* Japan must base her claims either on the Convention with China or on the right of conquest, or on both. Let us consider her moral right under either of these points.

"*a*) If the United States has not before this recognized the validity of the rights claimed by Japan under her Convention with China, what has happened since the Armistice that would justify us in recognizing their validity now?

"*b*) If Germany had possessed territory, in full sovereignty, on the east coast of Asia, a right to this territory, under international law, could have been obtained by conquest. But Germany possessed no such territory. What then was left for Japan to acquire by conquest? Apparently nothing but a lease extorted under compulsion from China by Germany. I understand that international lawyers hold that such a lease, or the rights acquired, justly or unjustly, under it, cannot be acquired by conquest.

"*Third.* Suppose Germany says to us, 'We will cede our

lease and all rights under it, but we will cede them back to China.' Will we recognize the justice of Japan's claims to such an extent that we will threaten Germany with further war unless she cedes these rights to Japan rather than to China?

"Again, suppose that Germany, in her hopelessness of resistance to our demands, should sign without question a clause ceding these rights to Japan, even though we know that this is so wrong that we would not fight in order to compel Germany to do it, what moral justification would we have in making Germany do this?

"*Fourth*. Stripped of all words that befog the issue, would we not, under the guise of making a treaty with Germany, really be making a treaty with Japan by which we compel one of our Allies (China) to cede against her will these things to Japan? Would not this action be really more unjustifiable than the one which you have refused to be a party to on the Dalmatian Coast? Because, in the latter case, the territory in dispute did not belong to one of the Allies, but to one of the Central Powers; the question in Dalmatia is as to which of two friendly powers we shall give territory taken from an enemy power; in China the question is, shall we take certain claimed rights from one friendly power in order to give them to another friendly power.

"It would seem to be advisable to call particular attention to what the Japanese mean when they say that they will return Kiao-chow to China. They *do not* offer to return the railway, the mines or the port, i.e., Tsingtau. The leased territory included a portion of land on the north-east side of the entrance of the Bay and another on the south-west and some islands. It is a small territory. The 50 Kilometer Zone was not included. That was a *limitation* put upon the movement of German troops.

They could not go beyond the boundary of the zone. Within this zone China enjoyed all rights of sovereignty and administration.

"Japan's proposal to abandon the zone is somewhat of an impertinence, since she has violated it ever since she took possession. She kept troops all along the railway line until recently and insists on maintaining in the future a guard at Tsinan, 254 miles away. The zone would restrict her military movements, consequently she gives it up.

"The proposals she makes are (1) to open the whole bay. It is from 15 to 20 miles from the entrance to the northern shore of the bay. (2) To have a Japanese exclusive concession *at a place* to be designated by her, i.e., she can take just as much as she likes of the territory around the bay. It may be as large as the present leased territory, but more likely it will include only the best part of Tsingtau. What then does she give up? Nothing but such parts of the leased territory as are of no value.

"The operation then would amount chiefly to an exchange of two pieces of paper — one cancelling the lease for 78 years, the other granting a more valuable concession which would amount to a permanent title to the port. Why take two years to go through this operation?

"If it be right for a policeman, who recovers your purse, to keep the contents and claim that he has fulfilled his duty in returning the empty purse, then Japan's conduct may be tolerated.

"If it be right for Japan to annex the territory of an Ally, then it cannot be wrong for Italy to retain Fiume taken from the enemy.

"If we support Japan's claim, we abandon the democracy of China to the domination of the Prussianized militarism of Japan.

"We shall be sowing dragons' teeth.

"It can't be right to do wrong even to make peace. Peace is desirable, but there are things dearer than peace, justice and freedom.

"Sincerely yours

"THE PRESIDENT" "T. H. BLISS

I have not discussed certain modifications proposed by the Japanese delegates, since, as is clear from General Bliss's letter, they amounted to nothing and were merely a pretense of concession and without substantial value.

The day following the delivery of this letter to the President (April 30), by which he was fully advised of the attitude of General Bliss, Mr. White, and myself in regard to the Japanese claims, the Council of Four reached its final decision of the matter, in which necessarily Mr. Wilson acquiesced. I learned of this decision the same evening. The memorandum which I made the next morning in regard to the matter is as follows:

"China has been abandoned to Japanese rapacity. A democratic territory has been given over to an autocratic government. The President has conceded to Japan all that, if not more than, she ever hoped to obtain. This is the information contained in a memorandum handed by Ray Stannard Baker under the President's direction to the Chinese delegation last evening, a copy of which reached me through Mr. —— [of the Chinese delegation].

"Mr. —— also said that Mr. Baker stated that the President desired him to say that the President was very sorry that he had not been able to do more for China but that he had been compelled to accede to Japan's demand 'in order *to save the League of Nations.*'

"The memorandum was most depressing. Though I had anticipated something of the sort three days ago [see note of April 28 previously quoted], I had unconsciously cherished a hope that the President would stand to his guns and champion China's cause. He has failed to do so. It is true that China is given the shell called 'sovereignty,' but the economic control, the kernel, is turned over to Japan.

"However logical may appear the argument that China's political integrity is preserved and will be maintained under the guaranty of the League of Nations, the fact is that Japan will rule over millions of Chinese. Furthermore it is still a matter of conjecture how valuable the guaranty of the League will prove to be. It has, of course, never been tried, and Japan's representation on the Council will possibly thwart any international action in regard to China.

"Frankly my policy would have been to say to the Japanese, 'If you do not give back to China what Germany stole from her, we don't want you in the League of Nations.' If the Japanese had taken offense and gone, I would have welcomed it, for we would have been well rid of a government with such imperial designs. But she would not have gone. She would have submitted. She has attained a high place in world councils. Her astute statesmen would never have abandoned her present exalted position even for the sake of Kiao-Chau. The whole affair assumes a sordid and sinister character, in which the President, acting undoubtedly with the best of motives, became the cat's-paw.

"I have no doubt that the President fully believed that the League of Nations was in jeopardy and that to save it he was compelled to subordinate every other consideration. The result was that China was offered up as a sacrifice to propitiate the threatening Moloch of Japan. When you get down to facts the threats were nothing but 'bluff.'

"I do not think that anything that has happened here has caused more severe or more outspoken criticism than this affair. I am heartsick over it, because I see how much good-will and regard the President is bound to lose. I can offer no adequate explanation to the critics. There seems to be none."

It is manifest, from the foregoing recital of events leading up to the decision in regard to the Shantung Question and the apparent reasons for the President's agreement to support the Japanese claims, that we radically differed as to the decision which was embodied in Articles 156, 157, and 158 of the Treaty of Versailles (see Appendix VI, p. 318). I do not think that we held different opinions as to the justice of the Chinese position, though probably the soundness of the legal argument in favor of the extinguishment of the German rights appealed more strongly to me than it did to Mr. Wilson. Our chief differences were, first, that it was more important to insure the acceptance of the Covenant of the League of Nations than to do strict justice to China; second, that the Japanese withdrawal from the Conference would prevent the formation of the League; and, third, that Japan would have withdrawn if her claims had been denied. As to these differences our opposite views remained unchanged after the Treaty of Versailles was signed.

When I was summoned before the Senate Committee on Foreign Relations on August 6, 1919, I told the Committee that, in my opinion, the Japanese signatures would have been affixed to the Treaty containing the Covenant even though Shantung had not been delivered over to Japan, and that the only reason that I had yielded was because it was my duty to follow the decision of the President of the United States.

About two weeks later, August 19, the President had a conference at the White House with the same Committee. In answer to questions regarding the Shantung Settlement, Mr. Wilson said concerning my statement that his judgment was different from mine, that in his judgment the signatures could not have been obtained if he had not given Shantung to Japan, and that he had been notified that the Japanese delegates had been instructed not to sign the Treaty unless the cession of the German rights in Shantung to Japan was included.

Presumably the opinion which Mr. Wilson held in the summer of 1919 he continues to hold, and for my part my views and feelings remain the same now as they were then, with possibly the difference that the indignation and shame that I felt at the time in being in any way a participant in robbing China of her just rights have increased rather than lessened.

So intense was the bitterness among the American Commissioners over the flagrant wrong being perpetrated that, when the decision of the Council of Four was known, some of them considered whether or not they ought to resign or give notice that they would not sign the Treaty if the

articles concerning Shantung appeared. The presence
at Versailles of the German plenipotentiaries, the uncertainty of the return of the Italian delegates then in Rome,
and the murmurs of dissatisfaction among the delegates of
the lesser nations made the international situation precarious. To have added to the serious conditions and to have
possibly precipitated a crisis by openly rebelling against
the President was to assume a responsibility which no
Commissioner was willing to take. With the greatest reluctance the American Commissioners submitted to the
decision of the Council of Four; and, when the Chinese
delegates refused to sign the Treaty after they had been
denied the right to sign it with reservations to the Shantung articles, the American Commissioners, who had so
strongly opposed the settlement, silently approved their
conduct as the only patriotic and statesmanlike course to
take. So far as China was concerned the Shantung Question remained open, and the Chinese Government very
properly refused, after the Treaty of Versailles was signed,
to enter into any negotiations with Japan looking toward
its settlement upon the basis of the treaty provisions.

There was one exception to the President's usual practice which is especially noticeable in connection with the
Shantung controversy, and that was the greater participation which he permitted the members of the American
Commission in negotiating with both the Japanese and
the Chinese. It is true he did not disclose his intentions to
the Commissioners, but he did express a wish for their ad-

vice and he directed me to confer with the Japanese and obtain their views. Just why he adopted this course, for him unusual, I do not know unless he felt that so far as the equity of China's claim was concerned we were all in agreement, and if there was to be a departure from strict justice he desired to have his colleagues suggest a way to do so. It is possible, too, that he felt the question was in large measure a legal one, and decided that the illegality of transferring the German rights to Japan could be more successfully presented to the Japanese delegates by a lawyer. In any event, in this particular case he adopted a course more in accord with established custom and practice than he did in any other of the many perplexing and difficult problems which he was called upon to solve during the Paris negotiations, excepting of course the subjects submitted to commissions of the Conference. As has been shown, Mr. Wilson did not follow the advice of the three Commissioners given him in General Bliss's letter, but that does not detract from the noteworthiness of the fact that in the case of Shantung he sought advice from his Commissioners.

This ends the account of the Shantung Settlement and the negotiations which led up to it. The consequences were those which were bound to follow so indefensible a decision as the one that was reached. Public opinion in the United States was almost unanimous in condemning it and in denouncing those responsible for so evident a departure from legal justice and the principles of international mo-

rality. No plea of expediency or of necessity excused such
a flagrant denial of undoubted right. The popular recognition that a great wrong had been done to a nation weak
because of political discord and an insufficient military establishment, in order to win favor with a nation strong because of its military power and national unity, had much
to do with increasing the hostility to the Treaty and preventing its acceptance by the Senate of the United States.
The whole affair furnishes another example of the results
of secret diplomacy, for the arguments which prevailed
with the President were those to which he listened when he
sat in secret council with M. Clemenceau and Mr. Lloyd
George.

CHAPTER XIX

THE BULLITT AFFAIR

THE foregoing chapters have related to subjects which were known to President Wilson to be matters of difference between us while we were together in Paris and which are presumably referred to in his letter of February 11, 1920, extracts from which are quoted in the opening chapter. The narration might be concluded with our difference of opinion as to the Shantung Settlement, but in view of subsequent information which the President received I am convinced that he felt that my objections to his decisions in regard to the terms of the peace with Germany extended further than he knew at the time, and that he resented the fact that my mind did not go along with his as to these decisions. This undoubtedly added to the reasons for his letter and possibly influenced him to write as he did in February, 1920, even more than our known divergence of judgment during the negotiations.

I do not feel, therefore, that the story is complete without at least a brief reference to my views concerning the Treaty of Versailles at the time of its delivery to the German delegates, which were imperfectly disclosed in a statement made by William C. Bullitt on September 12, 1919, at a public hearing before the Senate Committee on Foreign Relations. As to the conduct of Mr. Bullitt, who had held a responsible position with the American Commission at Paris, in voluntarily repeating a conversation which was from its nature highly confidential, I make no comment.

The portion of the statement, which I have no doubt deeply incensed the President because it was published while he was in the West making his appeals to the people in behalf of the Treaty and especially of the League of Nations, is as follows:

"Mr. Lansing said that he, too, considered many parts of the Treaty thoroughly bad, particularly those dealing with Shantung and the League of Nations. He said: 'I consider that the League of Nations at present is entirely useless. The Great Powers have simply gone ahead and arranged the world to suit themselves. England and France have gotten out of the Treaty everything that they wanted, and the League of Nations can do nothing to alter any of the unjust clauses of the Treaty except by unanimous consent of the members of the League, and the Great Powers will never give their consent to changes in the interests of weaker peoples.'

"We then talked about the possibility of ratification by the Senate. Mr. Lansing said: 'I believe that if the Senate could only understand what this Treaty means, and if the American people could really understand, it would unquestionably be defeated, but I wonder if they will ever understand what it lets them in for.'" (Senate Doc. 106, 66th Congress, 1st Session, p. 1276.)

It does not seem an unwarranted conjecture that the President believed that this statement, which was asserted by Mr. Bullitt to be from a memorandum made at the time, indicated that I had been unfaithful to him. He may even have concluded that I had been working against the League of Nations with the intention of bringing about the rejection of the Covenant by the Senate. If he did believe this, I cannot feel that it was other than natural in the circumstances, especially if I did not at once publicly deny the truth of the Bullitt statement. That I could not do because there was sufficient truth in it to compel me to show how, by slight variations and by omissions in the conversation, my words were misunderstood or misinterpreted.

In view of the fact that I found it impossible to make an absolute denial, I telegraphed the President stating the facts and offering to make them public if he considered it wise to do so. The important part of the telegram, which was dated September 16, 1919, is as follows:

"On May 17th Bullitt resigned by letter giving his reasons, with which you are familiar. I replied by letter on the 18th without any comment on his reasons. Bullitt on the 19th asked to see me to say good-bye and I saw him. He elaborated on the reasons for his resignation and said that he could not conscientiously give countenance to a treaty which was based on injustice. I told him that I would say nothing against his resigning since he put it on conscientious grounds, and that I recognized that certain features of the Treaty were bad, as I presumed most every one did, but that was probably unavoidable in view of conflicting claims and that nothing ought to be done to prevent the speedy restoration of peace by signing the Treaty. Bullitt then discussed the numerous European commissions provided for by the Treaty on which the United States was to be represented. I told him that I was disturbed by this fact because I was afraid the Senate and possibly the people, if they understood this, would refuse ratification, and that anything which was an obstacle to ratification was unfortunate because we ought to have peace as soon as possible."

It is very easy to see how by making a record of one side of this conversation without reference to the other side and by an omission here and there, possibly unintentionally, the sense was altered. Thus Mr. Bullitt, by repeating only a part of my words and by omitting the context, entirely changed the meaning of what was said. My attitude was, and I intended to show it at the time, that the Treaty should be signed and ratified at the earliest possible moment because the restoration of peace was paramount and that any provision in the Treaty which might delay the peace, by making uncertain senatorial consent to ratification, was to be deplored.

Having submitted to the President the question of making a public explanation of my interview with Mr. Bullitt which would in a measure at least correct the impression caused by his statement, I could not do so until I received the President's approval. That was never received. The telegram, which was sent to Mr. Wilson, through the Department of State, was never answered. It was not even acknowledged. The consequence was that the version of the conversation given by Mr. Bullitt was the only one that up to the present time has been published.

The almost unavoidable conclusion from the President's silence is that he considered my explanation was insufficient to destroy or even to weaken materially the effect of Mr. Bullitt's account of what had taken place, and that the public would believe in spite of it that I was opposed to the Treaty and hostile to the League of Nations. I am not disposed to blame the President for holding this opinion considering what had taken place at Paris. From his point of view a statement, such as I was willing to make, would in no way help the situation. I would still be on record as opposed to certain provisions of the Treaty, provisions which he was so earnestly defending in his addresses. While Mr. Bullitt had given an incomplete report of our conversation, there was sufficient truth in it to make anything but a flat denial seem of little value to the President; and, as I could not make such a denial, his point of view seemed to be that the damage was done and could not be undone. I am inclined to think that he was right.

My views concerning the Treaty at the time of the conversation with Mr. Bullitt are expressed in a memorandum of May 8, 1919, which is as follows:

"The terms of peace were yesterday delivered to the German plenipotentiaries, and for the first time in these days of feverish rush of preparation there is time to consider the Treaty as a complete document.

"The impression made by it is one of disappointment, of regret, and of depression. The terms of peace appear immeasurably harsh and humiliating, while many of them seem to me impossible of performance.

"The League of Nations created by the Treaty is relied upon to preserve the artificial structure which has been erected by compromise of the conflicting interests of the Great Powers and to prevent the germination of the seeds of war which are sown in so many articles and which under normal conditions would soon bear fruit. The League might as well attempt to prevent the growth of plant life in a tropical jungle. Wars will come sooner or later.

"It must be admitted in honesty that the League is an instrument of the mighty to check the normal growth of national power and national aspirations among those who have been rendered impotent by defeat. Examine the Treaty and you will find peoples delivered against their wills into the hands of those whom they hate, while their economic resources are torn from them and given to others. Resentment and bitterness, if not desperation, are bound to be the consequences of such provisions. It may be years before these oppressed peoples are able to throw off the yoke, but as sure as day follows night the time will come when they will make the effort.

"This war was fought by the United States to destroy forever the conditions which produced it. Those conditions have not been destroyed. They have been supplanted by other conditions equally productive of hatred, jealousy, and suspicion. In place of the Triple Alliance and the Entente has arisen the Quintuple Alliance which is to rule the world. The victors in this war intend to impose their combined will upon the vanquished and to subordinate all interests to their own.

"It is true that to please the aroused public opinion of mankind and to respond to the idealism of the moralist they have surrounded the new alliance with a halo and called it 'The League of Nations,' but whatever it may be called or however it may be disguised it is an alliance of the Five Great Military Powers.

"It is useless to close our eyes to the fact that the power to compel obedience by the exercise of the united strength of 'The Five' is the fundamental principle of the League. Justice is secondary. Might is primary.

"The League as now constituted will be the prey of greed and intrigue; and the law of unanimity in the Council, which may offer a restraint, will be broken or render the organization powerless. It is called upon to stamp as just what is unjust.

"We have a treaty of peace, but it will not bring permanent peace because it is founded on the shifting sands of self-interest."

In the views thus expressed I was not alone. A few days after they were written I was in London where I discussed the Treaty with several of the leading British statesmen. I noted their opinions thus: "The consensus was that the Treaty was unwise and unworkable, that it was conceived in intrigue and fashioned in cupidity, and that it would produce rather than prevent wars." One of these leaders of political thought in Great Britain said that "the only apparent purpose of the League of Nations seems to be to perpetuate the series of unjust provisions which were being imposed."

The day following my return from London, which was on May 17, I received Mr. Bullitt's letter of resignation and also letters from five of our principal experts protesting against the terms of peace and stating that they considered them to be an abandonment of the principles for which Americans had fought. One of the officials, whose relations with the President were of a most intimate nature, said that he was in a quandary about resigning; that he did not think that the conditions in the Treaty would make for peace because they were too oppressive; that the obnoxious things in the Treaty were due to secret diplomacy; and that the President should have stuck rigidly to his principles, which he had not. This official was evidently deeply incensed, but in the end he did not resign, nor did the five experts who sent letters, because they were told that it would seriously cripple the American Commission in the preparation of the Austrian Treaty if they did not continue to serve. Another and more prominent adviser of the President felt very bitterly over the terms of peace. In speaking of his disapproval of them he told me that he had found the same feeling among the British in Paris, who were disposed to blame the President since "they had counted upon him to stand firmly by his principles and face down the intriguers."

It is needless to cite other instances indicating the general state of mind among the Americans and British at Paris to show the views that were being exchanged and the frank comments that were being made at the time of my interview with Mr. Bullitt. In truth I said less to him in criticism of the Treaty than I did to some others, but they have seen fit to respect the confidential nature of our conversations.

It is not pertinent to the present subject to recite the

events between the delivery of the Treaty to the Germans on May 7 and its signature on June 28. In spite of the dissatisfaction, which even went so far that some of the delegates of the Great Powers threatened to decline to sign the Treaty unless certain of its terms were modified, the supreme necessity of restoring peace as soon as possible overcame all obstacles. It was the appreciation of this supreme necessity which caused many Americans to urge consent to ratification when the Treaty was laid before the Senate.

My own position was paradoxical. I was opposed to the Treaty, but signed it and favored its ratification. The explanation is this: Convinced after conversations with the President in July and August, 1919, that he would not consent to any effective reservations, the politic course seemed to be to endeavor to secure ratification without reservations. It appeared to be the only possible way of obtaining that for which all the world longed and which in the months succeeding the signature appeared absolutely essential to prevent the widespread disaster resulting from political and economic chaos which seemed to threaten many nations if not civilization itself. Even if the Treaty was bad in certain provisions, so long as the President remained inflexible and insistent, its ratification without change seemed a duty to humanity. At least that was my conviction in the summer and autumn of 1919, and I am not yet satisfied that it was erroneous. My views after January, 1920, are not pertinent to the subject under consideration. The consequences of the failure to ratify promptly the Treaty of Versailles are still uncertain. They may be more serious or they may be less serious than they appeared in 1919. Time alone will disclose the truth and fix the responsibility for what occurred after the Treaty of Versailles was laid before the Senate of the United States.

CONCLUSION

THE narration of my relations to the peace negotiations as one of the American Commissioners to the Paris Conference, which has been confined within the limits laid down in the opening chapter of this volume, concludes with the recital of the views which I held concerning the terms of the Treaty of Peace with Germany and which were brought to the attention of Mr. Wilson through the press reports of William C. Bullitt's statement to the Senate Committee on Foreign Relations on September 12, 1919.

The endeavor has been to present, as fully as possible in the circumstances, a review of my association with President Wilson in connection with the negotiations at Paris setting forth our differences of opinion and divergence of judgment upon the subjects coming before the Peace Conference, the conduct of the proceedings, and the terms of peace imposed upon Germany by the Treaty of Versailles.

It is evident from this review that, from a time prior to Mr. Wilson's departure from the United States on December 4, 1918, to attend the Peace Conference up to the delivery of the text of the Treaty to the German plenipotentiaries on May 7, 1919, there were many subjects of disagreement between the President and myself; that he was disposed to reject or ignore the advice and suggestions which I volunteered; and that in consequence of my convictions I followed his guidance and obeyed his instructions unwillingly.

While there were other matters of friction between us they were of a personal nature and of minor importance. Though they may have contributed to the formality of our relations they played no real part in the increasing difficulty of the situation. The matters narrated were, in my opinion, the principal causes for the letters written by President Wilson in February, 1920; at least they seem sufficient to explain the origin of the correspondence, while the causes specifically stated by him — my calling together of the heads of the executive departments for consultation during his illness and my attempts to anticipate his judgment — are insufficient.

The reasons given in the President's letter of February 11, the essential portions of which have been quoted, for stating that my resignation as Secretary of State would be acceptable to him, are the embarrassment caused him by my "reluctance and divergence of judgment" and the implication that my mind did not "willingly go along" with his. As neither of these reasons applies to the calling of Cabinet meetings or to the anticipation of his judgment in regard to foreign affairs, the unavoidable conclusion is that these grounds of complaint were not the real causes leading up to the severance of our official association.

The real causes — which are the only ones worthy of

consideration — are to be found in the record of the relations between President Wilson and myself in connection
with the peace negotiations. Upon that record must rest
the justification or the refutation of Mr. Wilson's implied
charge that I was not entirely loyal to him as President
and that I failed to perform my full duty to my country
as Secretary of State and as a Commissioner to Negotiate
Peace by opposing the way in which he exercised his constitutional authority to conduct the foreign affairs of the
United States.

THE END

APPENDIX I

THE PRESIDENT'S ORIGINAL DRAFT OF THE COVE-
NANT OF THE LEAGUE OF NATIONS, LAID BEFORE
THE AMERICAN COMMISSION ON JANUARY 10, 1919

PREAMBLE

IN order to secure peace, security, and orderly government
by the prescription of open, just, and honorable relations
between nations, by the firm establishment of the understandings of international law as the actual rule of conduct among governments, and by the maintenance of
justice and a scrupulous respect for all treaty obligations
in the dealings of organized peoples with one another, the
Powers signatory to this covenant and agreement jointly
and severally adopt this constitution of the League of
Nations.

ARTICLE I

THE action of the Signatory Powers under the terms of this
agreement shall be effected through the instrumentality
of a Body of Delegates which shall consist of the ambas-
sadors and ministers of the contracting Powers accredited to H. and the Minister for Foreign Affairs of H. The
meetings of the Body of Delegates shall be held at the seat
of government of H. and the Minister for Foreign Affairs
of H. shall be the presiding officer of the Body.

Whenever the Delegates deem it necessary or advisable,
they may meet temporarily at the seat of government of
B. or of S., in which case the Ambassador or Minister to
H. of the country in which the meeting is held shall be the
presiding officer *pro tempore*.

It shall be the privilege of any of the contracting Powers to assist its representative in the Body of Delegates by any method of conference, counsel, or advice that may seem best to it, and also to substitute upon occasion a special representative for its regular diplomatic representative accredited to H.

ARTICLE II

THE Body of Delegates shall regulate their own procedure and shall have power to appoint such committees as they may deem necessary to inquire into and report upon any matters that lie within the field of their action.

It shall be the right of the Body of Delegates, upon the initiative of any member, to discuss, either publicly or privately as it may deem best, any matter lying within the jurisdiction of the League of Nations as defined in this Covenant, or any matter likely to affect the peace of the world; but all actions of the Body of Delegates taken in the exercise of the functions and powers granted to them under this Covenant shall be first formulated and agreed upon by an Executive Council, which shall act either by reference or upon its own initiative and which shall consist of the representatives of the Great Powers together with representatives drawn in annual rotation from two panels, one of which shall be made up of the representatives of the States ranking next after the Great Powers and the other of the representatives of the minor States (a classification which the Body of Delegates shall itself establish and may from time to time alter), such a number being drawn from these panels as will be but one less than the representatives of the Great Powers; and three or more negative votes in the Council shall operate as a veto upon any action or resolution proposed.

All resolutions passed or actions taken by the Body of

Delegates upon the recommendation of the Executive Council, except those adopted in execution of any direct powers herein granted to the Body of Delegates themselves, shall have the effect of recommendations to the several governments of the League.

The Executive Council shall appoint a permanent Secretariat and staff and may appoint joint committees chosen from the Body of Delegates or consisting of specially qualified persons outside of that Body, for the study and systematic consideration of the international questions with which the Council may have to deal, or of questions likely to lead to international complications or disputes. It shall also take the necessary steps to establish and maintain proper liaison both with the foreign offices of the signatory powers and with any governments or agencies which may be acting as mandatories of the League of Nations in any part of the world.

ARTICLE III

THE Contracting Powers unite in guaranteeing to each other political independence and territorial integrity; but it is understood between them that such territorial readjustments, if any, as may in the future become necessary by reason of changes in present racial conditions and aspirations or present social and political relationships, pursuant to the principle of self-determination, and also such territorial readjustments as may in the judgment of three fourths of the Delegates be demanded by the welfare and manifest interest of the peoples concerned, may be effected if agreeable to those peoples; and that territorial changes may in equity involve material compensation. The Contracting Powers accept without reservation the principle that the peace of the world is superior in importance to every question of political jurisdiction or boundary.

Article IV

The Contracting Powers recognize the principle that the establishment and maintenance of peace will require the reduction of national armaments to the lowest point consistent with domestic safety and the enforcement by common action of international obligations; and the Delegates are directed to formulate at once plans by which such a reduction may be brought about. The plan so formulated shall be binding when, and only when, unanimously approved by the Governments signatory to this Covenant.

As the basis for such a reduction of armaments, all the Powers subscribing to the Treaty of Peace of which this Covenant constitutes a part hereby agree to abolish conscription and all other forms of compulsory military service, and also agree that their future forces of defence and of international action shall consist of militia or volunteers, whose numbers and methods of training shall be fixed, after expert inquiry, by the agreements with regard to the reduction of armaments referred to in the last preceding paragraph.

The Body of Delegates shall also determine for the consideration and action of the several governments what direct military equipment and armament is fair and reasonable in proportion to the scale of forces laid down in the programme of disarmament; and these limits, when adopted, shall not be exceeded without the permission of the Body of Delegates.

The Contracting Powers further agree that munitions and implements of war shall not be manufactured by private enterprise or for private profit, and that there shall be full and frank publicity as to all national armaments and military or naval programmes.

Article V

THE Contracting Powers jointly and severally agree that, should disputes or difficulties arise between or among them which cannot be satisfactorily settled or adjusted by the ordinary processes of diplomacy, they will in no case resort to armed force without previously submitting the questions and matters involved either to arbitration or to inquiry by the Executive Council of the Body of Delegates or until there has been an award by the arbitrators or a decision by the Executive Council; and that they will not even then resort to armed force as against a member of the League of Nations who complies with the award of the arbitrators or the decision of the Executive Council.

The Powers signatory to this Covenant undertake and agree that whenever any dispute or difficulty shall arise between or among them with regard to any questions of the law of nations, with regard to the interpretation of a treaty, as to any fact which would, if established, constitute a breach of international obligation, or as to any alleged damage and the nature and measure of the reparation to be made therefor, if such dispute or difficulty cannot be satisfactorily settled by the ordinary processes of negotiation, to submit the whole subject-matter to arbitration and to carry out in full good faith any award or decision that may be rendered.

In case of arbitration, the matter or matters at issue shall be referred to three arbitrators, one of the three to be selected by each of the parties to the dispute, when there are but two such parties, and the third by the two thus selected. When there are more than two parties to the dispute, one arbitrator shall be named by each of the several parties, and the arbitrators thus named shall add to their number others of their own choice, the number thus added to be limited to the number which will suffice to give a deciding voice to the arbitrators thus added in case of a tie vote among the arbitrators chosen by the contending parties. In case the arbitrators chosen by the contending parties cannot agree upon an additional arbitrator or arbitrators, the additional arbitrator or arbitrators shall be chosen by the Body of Delegates.

On the appeal of a party to the dispute the decision of the arbitrators may be set aside by a vote of three-fourths of the Delegates, in case the decision of the arbitrators was unanimous, or by a vote of two-thirds of the Delegates in case the decision of the arbitrators was not unanimous, but unless thus set aside shall be finally binding and conclusive.

When any decision of arbitrators shall have been thus set aside, the dispute shall again be submitted to arbitrators chosen as heretofore provided, none of whom shall, however, have previously acted as arbitrators in the dispute in question, and the decision of the arbitrators rendered in this second arbitration shall be finally binding and conclusive without right of appeal.

If for any reason it should prove impracticable to refer any matter in dispute to arbitration, the parties to the dispute shall apply to the Executive Council to take the matter under consideration for such mediatory action or recommendation as it may deem wise in the circumstances. The Council shall immediately accept the reference and give notice to the other party or parties, and shall make the necessary arrangements for a full hearing, investigation, and consideration. It shall ascertain all the facts involved in the dispute and shall make such recommendations as it may deem wise and practicable based on the merits of the controversy and calculated to secure a just and lasting settlement. Other members of the League shall place at the disposal of the Executive Council any and all information that may be in their possession which in any way bears upon the facts or merits of the controversy; and the Executive Council shall do everything in its power by way of mediation or conciliation to bring about a peaceful settlement. The decisions of the Executive Council shall be addressed to the disputants, and shall not have the force of a binding verdict. Should the Executive Council fail to arrive at any conclusion, it shall be the privilege of the members of the Executive Council to publish their several conclusions or recommendations; and such publications shall not be regarded as an unfriendly act by either or any of the disputants.

Article VI

Should any contracting Power break or disregard its covenants under Article V, it shall thereby *ipso facto* commit an act of war with all the members of the League, which shall immediately subject it to a complete economic and financial boycott, including the severance of all trade or financial relations, the prohibition of all intercourse between their subjects and the subjects of the covenant-breaking State, and the prevention, so far as possible, of all financial, commercial, or personal intercourse between the subjects of the covenant-breaking State and the subjects of any other State, whether a member of the League of Nations or not.

It shall be the privilege and duty of the Executive Council of the Body of Delegates in such a case to recommend what effective military or naval force the members of the League of Nations shall severally contribute, and to advise, if it should think best, that the smaller members of the League be excused from making any contribution to the armed forces to be used against the covenant-breaking State.

The covenant-breaking State shall, after the restoration of peace, be subject to perpetual disarmament and to the regulations with regard to a peace establishment provided for new States under the terms of SUPPLEMENTARY ARTICLE IV.

ARTICLE VII

IF any Power shall declare war or begin hostilities, or take any hostile step short of war, against another Power before submitting the dispute involved to arbitrators or consideration by the Executive Council as herein provided, or shall declare war or begin hostilities, or take any hostile step short of war, in regard to any dispute which has been decided adversely to it by arbitrators chosen and empowered as herein provided, the Contracting Powers hereby bind themselves not only to cease all commerce and intercourse with that Power but also to unite in blockading and closing the frontiers of that Power to commerce or intercourse with any part of the world and to use any force that may be necessary to accomplish that object.

ARTICLE VIII

ANY war or threat of war, whether immediately affecting any of the Contracting Powers or not, is hereby declared a matter of concern to the League of Nations and to all the Powers signatory hereto, and those Powers hereby reserve the right to take any action that may be deemed wise and effectual to safeguard the peace of nations.

It is hereby also declared and agreed to be the friendly right of each of the nations signatory or adherent to this Covenant to draw the attention of the Body of Delegates to any circumstances anywhere which threaten to disturb international peace or the good understanding between nations upon which peace depends.

The Delegates shall meet in the interest of peace whenever war is rumored or threatened, and also whenever the Delegate of any Power shall inform the Delegates that a meeting and conference in the interest of peace is advisable.

The Delegates may also meet at such other times and upon such other occasions as they shall from time to time deem best and determine.

ARTICLE IX

IN the event of a dispute arising between one of the Contracting Powers and a Power not a party to this Covenant, the Contracting Power involved hereby binds itself to endeavour to obtain the submission of the dispute to judicial decision or to arbitration. If the other Power will not agree to submit the dispute to judicial decision or to arbitration, the Contracting Power shall bring the matter to the attention of the Body of Delegates. The Delegates shall in such a case, in the name of the League of Nations, invite the Power not a party to this Covenant to become *ad hoc* a party and to submit its case to judicial decision or to arbitration, and if that Power consents it is hereby agreed that the provisions hereinbefore contained and applicable to the submission of disputes to arbitration or discussion shall be in all respects applicable to the dispute both in favour of and against such Power as if it were a party to this Covenant.

In case the Power not a party to this Covenant shall not accept the invitation of the Delegates to become *ad hoc* a party, it shall be the duty of the Executive Council immediately to institute an inquiry into the circumstances and merits of the dispute involved and to recommend such joint action by the Contracting Powers as may seem best and most effectual in the circumstances disclosed.

ARTICLE X

IF hostilities should be begun or any hostile action taken against the Contracting Power by the Power not a party to this Covenant before a decision of the dispute by arbitrators or before investigation, report and recommendation by the Executive Council in regard to the dispute, or contrary to such recommendation, the Contracting Powers shall thereupon cease all commerce and communication with that Power and shall also unite in blockading and closing the frontiers of that Power to all commerce or intercourse with any part of the world, employing jointly any force that may be necessary to accomplish that object. The Contracting Powers shall also unite in coming to the assistance of the Contracting Power against which hostile action has been taken, combining their armed forces in its behalf.

ARTICLE XI

IN case of a dispute between states not parties to this Covenant, any Contracting Power may bring the matter to the attention of the Delegates, who shall thereupon tender the good offices of the League of Nations with a view to the peaceable settlement of the dispute.

If one of the states, a party to the dispute, shall offer and agree to submit its interests and causes of action wholly to the control and decision of the League of Nations, that state shall *ad hoc* be deemed a Contracting Power. If no one of the states, parties to the dispute, shall so offer and agree, the Delegates shall, through the Executive Council, of their own motion take such action and make such recommendation to their governments as will prevent hostilities and result in the settlement of the dispute.

Article XII

Any Power not a party to this Covenant, whose government is based upon the principle of popular self-government, may apply to the Body of Delegates for leave to become a party. If the Delegates shall regard the granting thereof as likely to promote the peace, order, and security of the World, they may act favourably on the application, and their favourable action shall operate to constitute the Power so applying in all respects a full signatory party to this Covenant. This action shall require the affirmative vote of two-thirds of the Delegates.

Article XIII

The Contracting Powers severally agree that the present Covenant and Convention is accepted as abrogating all treaty obligations *inter se* which are inconsistent with the terms hereof, and solemnly engage that they will not enter into any engagements inconsistent with the terms hereof.

In case any of the Powers signatory hereto or subsequently admitted to the League of Nations shall, before becoming a party to this Covenant, have undertaken any treaty obligations which are inconsistent with the terms of this Covenant, it shall be the duty of such Power to take immediate steps to procure its release from such obligations.

SUPPLEMENTARY AGREEMENTS

I

In respect of the peoples and territories which formerly belonged to Austria-Hungary, and to Turkey, and in respect of the colonies formerly under the dominion of the German Empire, the League of Nations shall be regarded as the residuary trustee with sovereign right of ultimate disposal or of continued administration in accordance with certain fundamental principles hereinafter set forth; and this reversion and control shall exclude all rights or privileges of annexation on the part of any Power.

These principles are, that there shall in no case be any annexation of any of these territories by any State either within the League or outside of it, and that in the future government of these peoples and territories the rule of self-determination, or the consent of the governed to their form of government, shall be fairly and reasonably applied, and all policies of administration or economic development be based primarily upon the well-considered interests of the people themselves.

II

ANY authority, control, or administration which may be necessary in respect of these peoples or territories other than their own self-determined and self-organized autonomy shall be the exclusive function of and shall be vested in the League of Nations and exercised or undertaken by or on behalf of it.

It shall be lawful for the League of Nations to delegate its authority, control, or administration of any such people or territory to some single State or organized agency which it may designate and appoint as its agent or mandatory; but whenever or wherever possible or feasible the agent or mandatory so appointed shall be nominated or approved by the autonomous people or territory.

III

THE degree of authority, control, or administration to be exercised by the mandatary State or agency shall in each case be explicitly defined by the League in a special Act or Charter which shall reserve to the League complete power of supervision and of intimate control, and which shall also reserve to the people of any such territory or governmental unit the right to appeal to the League for the redress or correction of any breach of the mandate by the mandatary State or agency or for the substitution of some other State or agency, as mandatary.

The mandatary State or agency shall in all cases be bound and required to maintain the policy of the open door, or equal opportunity for all the signatories to this Covenant, in respect of the use and development of the economic resources of such people or territory.

The mandatary State or agency shall in no case form or maintain any military or naval force in excess of definite standards laid down by the League itself for the purposes of internal police.

IV

No new State arising or created from the old Empires of Austria-Hungary, or Turkey shall be recognized by the League or admitted into its membership except on condition that its military and naval forces and armaments shall conform to standards prescribed by the League in respect of it from time to time.

As successor to the Empires, the League of Nations is empowered, directly and without right of delegation, to watch over the relations *inter se* of all new independent States arising or created out of the Empires, and shall assume and fulfill the duty of conciliating and composing differences between them with a view to the maintenance of settled order and the general peace.

V

THE Powers signatory or adherent to this Covenant agree that they will themselves seek to establish and maintain fair hours and humane conditions of labour for all those within their several jurisdictions who are engaged in manual labour and that they will exert their influence in favour of the adoption and maintenance of a similar policy and like safeguards wherever their industrial and commercial relations extend.

VI

THE League of Nations shall require all new States to bind themselves as a condition precedent to their recognition as independent or autonomous States, to accord to all racial or national minorities within their several jurisdictions exactly the same treatment and security, both in law and in fact, that is accorded the racial or national majority of their people.

APPENDIX II

LEAGUE OF NATIONS

(*Plan of Lord Robert Cecil*[1])

I

ORGANIZATION

THE general treaty setting up the league of nations will explicitly provide for regular conferences between the responsible representatives of the contracting powers.

These conferences would review the general conditions of international relations and would naturally pay special attention to any difficulty which might seem to threaten the peace of the world. They would also receive and as occasion demanded discuss reports as to the work of any international administrative or investigating bodies working under the League.

These conferences would constitute the pivot of the league. They would be meetings of statesmen responsible to their own sovereign parliaments, and any decisions taken would therefore, as in the case of the various allied conferences during the war, have to be unanimous.

The following form of organization is suggested:

1. *The conference.* Annual meeting of prime ministers and foreign secretaries of British Empire, United States, France, Italy, Japan, and any other States recognized by them as great powers. Quadrennial meeting of representatives of all States included in the league. There should also be provision for the summoning of special conferences

[1] Reprinted from Senate Doc. No. 106, 66th Congress, 1st Session, p. 1163.

on the demand of any one of the great powers or, if there were danger of an outbreak of war, of any member of the league. (The composition of the league will be determined at the peace conference. Definitely untrustworthy and hostile States, e.g., Russia, should the Bolshevist government remain in power, should be excluded. Otherwise it is desirable not to be too rigid in scrutinizing qualifications, since the small powers will in any case not exercise any considerable influence.)

2. For the conduct of its work the interstate conference will require a permanent secretariat. The general secretary should be appointed by the great powers, if possible choosing a national of some other country.

3. *International bodies.* The secretariat would be the responsible channel of communication between the interstate conference and all international bodies functioning under treaties guaranteed by the league. These would fall into three classes:

(*a*) Judicial; i.e., the existing Hague organization with any additions or modifications made by the league.

(*b*) International administrative bodies. Such as the suggested transit commission. To these would be added bodies already formed under existing treaties (which are very numerous and deal with very important interests, e.g., postal union, international labor office, etc.).

(*c*) International commissions of enquiry: e.g., commission on industrial conditions (labor legislation), African commission, armaments commission.

4. In addition to the above arrangements guaranteed by or arising out of the general treaty, there would probably be a periodical congress of delegates of the parliaments of the States belonging to the league, as a development out of the existing Interparliamentary Union. A regular staple of discussion for this body would be afforded

by the reports of the interstate conference and of the different international bodies. The congress would thus cover the ground that is at present occupied by the periodical Hague Conference and also the ground claimed by the Socialist International.

For the efficient conduct of all these activities it is essential that there should be a permanent central meeting-place, where the officials and officers of the league would enjoy the privileges of extra-territoriality. Geneva is suggested as the most suitable place.

II

PREVENTION OF WAR

THE covenants for the prevention of war which would be embodied in the general treaty would be as follows:

(1) The members of the league would bind themselves not to go to war until they had submitted the questions at issue to an international conference or an arbitral court, and until the conference or court had issued a report or handed down an award.

(2) The members of the league would bind themselves not to go to war with any member of the league complying with the award of a court or with the report of a conference. For the purpose of this clause, the report of the conference must be unanimous, excluding the litigants.

(3) The members of the league would undertake to regard themselves, as *ipso facto*, at war with any one of them acting contrary to the above covenants, and to take, jointly and severally, appropriate military, economic and other measure against the recalcitrant State.

(4) The members of the league would bind themselves to take similar action, in the sense of the above clause, against any State not being a member of the league which is involved in a dispute with a member of the league.

(This is a stronger provision than that proposed in the Phillimore Report.)

The above covenants mark an advance upon the practice of international relations previous to the war in two respects: (1) In insuring a necessary period of delay before war can break out (except between two States which are neither of them members of the league); (2) In securing public discussion and probably a public report upon matters in dispute.

It should be observed that even in cases where the conference report is not unanimous, and therefore in no sense binding, a majority report may be issued and that this would be likely to carry weight with the public opinion of the States in the league.

APPENDIX III

THE COVENANT OF THE LEAGUE OF NATIONS IN THE TREATY OF VERSAILLES

ARTICLE 1

THE original Members of the League of Nations shall be those of the Signatories which are named in the Annex to this Covenant and also such of those other States named in the Annex as shall accede without reservation to this Covenant. Such accession shall be effected by a Declaration deposited with the Secretariat within two months of the coming into force of the Covenant. Notice thereof shall be sent to all other Members of the League.

Any fully self-governing State, Dominion, or Colony not named in the Annex may become a Member of the League if its admission is agreed to by two thirds of the Assembly, provided that it shall give effective guarantees of its sincere intention to observe its international obligations, and shall accept such regulations as may be prescribed by the League in regard to its military, naval and air forces and armaments.

Any Member of the League may, after two years' notice of its intention so to do, withdraw from the League, provided that all its international obligations and all its obligations under this Covenant shall have been fulfilled at the time of its withdrawal.

ARTICLE 2

THE action of the League under this Covenant shall be effected through the instrumentality of an Assembly and of a Council, with a permanent Secretariat.

ARTICLE 3

THE Assembly shall consist of Representatives of the Members of the League.

The Assembly shall meet at stated intervals and from time to time as occasion may require at the Seat of the League or at such other place as may be decided upon.

The Assembly may deal at its meetings with any matter within the sphere of action of the League or affecting the peace of the world.

At meetings of the Assembly each Member of the League shall have one vote, and may have not more than three Representatives.

ARTICLE 4

THE Council shall consist of Representatives of the Principal Allied and Associated Powers, together with Representatives of four other Members of the League. These four Members of the League shall be selected by the Assembly from time to time in its discretion. Until the appointment of the Representatives of the four Members of the League first selected by the Assembly, Representatives of Belgium, Brazil, Spain, and Greece shall be members of the Council.

With the approval of the majority of the Assembly, the Council may name additional Members of the League whose Representatives shall always be members of the Council; the Council with like approval may increase the number of Members of the League to be selected by the Assembly for representation on the Council.

The Council shall meet from time to time as occasion may require, and at least once a year, at the Seat of the League, or at such other place as may be decided upon.

The Council may deal at its meetings with any matter

within the sphere of action of the League or affecting the peace of the world.

Any Member of the League not represented on the Council shall be invited to send a Representative to sit as a member at any meeting of the Council during the consideration of matters specially affecting the interests of that Member of the League.

At meetings of the Council, each Member of the League represented on the Council shall have one vote, and may have not more than one Representative.

ARTICLE 5

EXCEPT where otherwise expressly provided in this Covenant or by the terms of the present Treaty, decisions at any meeting of the Assembly or of the Council shall require the agreement of all the Members of the League represented at the meeting.

All matters of procedure at meetings of the Assembly or of the Council, including the appointment of Committees to investigate particular matters, shall be regulated by the Assembly or by the Council and may be decided by a majority of the Members of the League represented at the meeting.

The first meeting of the Assembly and the first meeting of the Council shall be summoned by the President of the United States of America.

ARTICLE 6

THE permanent Secretariat shall be established at the Seat of the League. The Secretariat shall comprise a Secretary General and such secretaries and staff as may be required.

The first Secretary General shall be the person named in the Annex; thereafter the Secretary General shall be appointed by the Council with the approval of the majority of the Assembly.

The secretaries and staff of the Secretariat shall be appointed by the Secretary General with the approval of the Council.

The Secretary General shall act in that capacity at all meetings of the Assembly and of the Council.

The expenses of the Secretariat shall be borne by the Members of the League in accordance with the apportionment of the expenses of the International Bureau of the Universal Postal Union.

ARTICLE 7

THE Seat of the League is established at Geneva.

The Council may at any time decide that the Seat of the League shall be established elsewhere.

All positions under or in connection with the League, including the Secretariat, shall be open equally to men and women.

Representatives of the Members of the League and officials of the League when engaged on the business of the League shall enjoy diplomatic privileges and immunities.

The buildings and other property occupied by the League or its officials or by Representatives attending its meetings shall be inviolable.

ARTICLE 8

THE Members of the League recognize that the maintenance of peace requires the reduction of national armaments to the lowest point consistent with national safety and the enforcement by common action of international obligations.

The Council, taking account of the geographical situation and circumstances of each State, shall formulate plans for such reduction for the consideration and action of the several Governments.

Such plans shall be subject to reconsideration and revision at least every ten years.

After these plans shall have been adopted by the several Governments, the limits of armaments therein fixed shall not be exceeded without the concurrence of the Council.

The Members of the League agree that the manufacture by private enterprise of munitions and implements of war is open to grave objections. The Council shall advise how the evil effects attendant upon such manufacture can be prevented, due regard being had to the necessities of those Members of the League which are not able to manufacture the munitions and implements of war necessary for their safety.

The Members of the League undertake to interchange full and frank information as to the scale of their armaments, their military, naval and air programmes and the condition of such of their industries as are adaptable to warlike purposes.

ARTICLE 9

A PERMANENT Commission shall be constituted to advise the Council on the execution of the provisions of Articles 1 and 8 and on military, naval and air questions generally.

ARTICLE 10

THE Members of the League undertake to respect and preserve as against external aggression the territorial integrity and existing political independence of all Members of the League. In case of any such aggression or in case of any threat or danger of such aggression the Council shall advise upon the means by which this obligation shall be fulfilled.

ARTICLE 11

ANY war or threat of war, whether immediately affecting any of the Members of the League or not, is hereby declared a matter of concern to the whole League, and the League shall take any action that may be deemed wise and effectual to safeguard the peace of nations. In case any such emergency should arise the Secretary General shall on the request of any Member of the League forthwith summon a meeting of the Council.

It is also declared to be the friendly right of each Member of the League to bring to the attention of the Assembly or of the Council any circumstance whatever affecting international relations which threatens to disturb international peace or the good understanding between nations upon which peace depends.

ARTICLE 12

THE Members of the League agree that if there should arise between them any dispute likely to lead to a rupture, they will submit the matter either to arbitration or to inquiry by the Council, and they agree in no case to resort to war until three months after the award by the arbitrators or the report by the Council.

In any case under this Article the award of the arbitrators shall be made within a reasonable time, and the report of the Council shall be made within six months after the submission of the dispute.

ARTICLE 13

THE Members of the League agree that whenever any dispute shall arise between them which they recognize to be suitable for submission to arbitration and which cannot be satisfactorily settled by diplomacy, they will submit the whole subject-matter to arbitration.

Disputes as to the interpretation of a treaty, as to any question of international law, as to the existence of any fact which if established would constitute a breach of any international obligation, or as to the extent and nature of the reparation to be made for any such breach, are declared to be among those which are generally suitable for submission to arbitration.

For the consideration of any such dispute the court of arbitration to which the case is referred shall be the Court agreed on by the parties to the dispute or stipulated in any convention existing between them.

The Members of the League agree that they will carry out in full good faith any award that may be rendered, and that they will not resort to war against a Member of the League which complies therewith. In the event of any failure to carry out such an award, the Council shall propose what steps should be taken to give effect thereto.

ARTICLE 14

THE Council shall formulate and submit to the Members of the League for adoption plans for the establishment of a Permanent Court of International Justice. The Court shall be competent to hear and determine any dispute of an international character which the parties thereto submit to it. The Court may also give an advisory opinion upon any dispute or question referred to it by the Council or by the Assembly.

ARTICLE 15

IF there should arise between Members of the League any dispute likely to lead to a rupture, which is not submitted to arbitration in accordance with Article 13, the Members of the League agree that they will submit the matter to the Council. Any party to the dispute may effect such submission by giving notice of the existence of the dispute to the Secretary General, who will make all necessary arrangements for a full investigation and consideration thereof.

For this purpose the parties to the dispute will communicate to the Secretary General, as promptly as possible, statements of their case with all the relevant facts and papers, and the Council may forthwith direct the publication thereof.

The Council shall endeavour to effect a settlement of the dispute, and if such efforts are successful, a statement shall be made public giving such facts and explanations regarding the dispute and the terms of settlement thereof as the Council may deem appropriate.

If the dispute is not thus settled, the Council either unanimously or by a majority vote shall make and publish a report containing a statement of the facts of the dispute and the recommendations which are deemed just and proper in regard thereto.

Any Member of the League represented on the Council may make public a statement of the facts of the dispute and of its conclusions regarding the same.

If a report by the Council is unanimously agreed to by the members thereof other than the Representatives of one or more of the parties to the dispute, the Members of the League agree that they will not go to war with any party to the dispute which complies with the recommendations of the report.

If the Council fails to reach a report which is unanimously agreed to by the members thereof, other than the Representatives of one or more of the parties to the dispute, the Members of the League reserve to themselves the right to take such action as they shall consider necessary for the maintenance of right and justice.

If the dispute between the parties is claimed by one of

them, and is found by the Council, to arise out of a matter which by international law is solely within the domestic jurisdiction of that party, the Council shall so report, and shall make no recommendation as to its settlement.

The Council may in any case under this Article refer the dispute to the Assembly. The dispute shall be so referred at the request of either party to the dispute, provided that such request be made within fourteen days after the submission of the dispute to the Council.

In any case referred to the Assembly, all the provisions of this Article and of Article 12 relating to the action and powers of the Council shall apply to the action and powers of the Assembly, provided that a report made by the Assembly, if concurred in by the Representatives of those Members of the League represented on the Council and of a majority of the other Members of the League, exclusive in each case of the Representatives of the parties to the dispute, shall have the same force as a report by the Council concurred in by all the members thereof other than the Representatives of one or more of the parties to the dispute.

ARTICLE 16

SHOULD any Member of the League resort to war in disregard of its covenants under Articles 12, 13 or 15, it shall *ipso facto* be deemed to have committed an act of war against all other Members of the League, which hereby undertake immediately to subject it to the severance of all trade or financial relations, the prohibition of all intercourse between their nationals and the nationals of the covenant-breaking State, and the prevention of all financial, commercial or personal intercourse between the nationals of the covenant-breaking State and the nationals of any other State, whether a Member of the League or not.

It shall be the duty of the Council in such case to recommend to the several Governments concerned what effective military, naval or air force the Members of the League shall severally contribute to the armed forces to be used to protect the covenants of the League.

The Members of the League agree, further, that they will mutually support one another in the financial and economic measures which are taken under this Article, in order to minimise the loss and inconvenience resulting from the above measures, and that they will mutually support one another in resisting any special measures aimed at one of their number by the covenant-breaking State, and that they will take the necessary steps to afford passage through their territory to the forces of any of the Members of the League which are coöperating to protect the covenants of the League.

Any Member of the League which has violated any covenant of the League may be declared to be no longer a Member of the League by a vote of the Council concurred in by the Representatives of all the other Members of the League represented thereon.

ARTICLE 17

IN the event of a dispute between a Member of the League and a State which is not a Member of the League, or between States not Members of the League, the State or States not Members of the League shall be invited to accept the obligations of membership in the League for the purposes of such dispute, upon such conditions as the Council may deem just. If such invitation is accepted, the provisions of Articles 12 to 16 inclusive shall be applied with such modifications as may be deemed necessary by the Council.

Upon such invitation being given the Council shall immediately institute an inquiry into the circumstances of the dispute and recommend such action as may seem best and most effectual in the circumstances.

If a State so invited shall refuse to accept the obligations of membership in the League for the purposes of such dispute, and shall resort to war against a Member of the League, the provisions of Article 16 shall be applicable as against the State taking such action.

If both parties to the dispute when so invited refuse to accept the obligations of membership in the League for the purposes of such dispute, the Council may take such measures and make such recommendations as will prevent hostilities and will result in the settlement of the dispute.

ARTICLE 18

EVERY treaty or international engagement entered into hereafter by any Member of the League shall be forthwith registered with the Secretariat and shall as soon as possible be published by it. No such treaty or international engagement shall be binding until so registered.

ARTICLE 19

THE Assembly may from time to time advise the reconsideration by Members of the League of treaties which have become inapplicable and the consideration of international conditions whose continuance might endanger the peace of the world.

ARTICLE 20

THE Members of the League severally agree that this Covenant is accepted as abrogating all obligations or understandings *inter se* which are inconsistent with the terms thereof, and solemnly undertake that they will not hereafter enter into any engagements inconsistent with the terms thereof.

In case any Member of the League shall, before becoming a Member of the League, have undertaken any obligations inconsistent with the terms of this Covenant, it shall be the duty of such Member to take immediate steps to procure its release from such obligations.

ARTICLE 21

NOTHING in this Covenant shall be deemed to affect the validity of international engagements, such as treaties of arbitration or regional understandings like the Monroe Doctrine, for securing the maintenance of peace.

ARTICLE 22

To those colonies and territories which as a consequence of the late war have ceased to be under the sovereignty of the States which formerly governed them and which are inhabited by peoples not yet able to stand by themselves under the strenuous conditions of the modern world, there should be applied the principle that the well-being and development of such peoples form a sacred trust of civilisation and that securities for the performance of this trust should be embodied in this Covenant.

The best method of giving practical effect to this principle is that the tutelage of such peoples should be entrusted to advanced nations who by reason of their resources, their experience or their geographical position can best undertake this responsibility, and who are willing to accept it, and that this tutelage should be exercised by them as Mandatories on behalf of the League.

The character of the mandate must differ according to the stage of the development of the people, the geographical situation of the territory, its economic conditions and other similar circumstances.

Certain communities formerly belonging to the Turkish

Empire have reached a stage of development where their existence as independent nations can be provisionally recognised subject to the rendering of administrative advice and assistance by a Mandatory until such time as they are able to stand alone. The wishes of these communities must be a principal consideration in the selection of the Mandatory.

Other peoples, especially those of Central Africa, are at such a stage that the Mandatory must be responsible for the administration of the territory under conditions which will guarantee freedom of conscience and religion, subject only to the maintenance of public order and morals, the prohibition of abuses such as the slave trade, the arms traffic and the liquor traffic, and the prevention of the establishment of fortifications or military and naval bases and of military training of the natives for other than police purposes and the defense of territory, and will also secure equal opportunities for the trade and commerce of other Members of the League.

There are territories, such as South-West Africa and certain of the South Pacific Islands, which, owing to the sparseness of their population, or their small size, or their remoteness from the centres of civilisation, or their geographical contiguity to the territory of the Mandatory, and other circumstances, can be best administered under the laws of the Mandatory as integral portions of its territory, subject to the safeguards above mentioned in the interests of the indigenous population.

In every case of mandate, the Mandatory shall render to the Council an annual report in reference to the territory committed to its charge.

The degree of authority, control, or administration to be exercised by the Mandatory shall, if not previously agreed upon by the Members of the League, be explicitly defined in each case by the Council.

A permanent Commission shall be constituted to receive and examine the annual reports of the Mandatories and to advise the Council on all matters relating to the observance of the mandates.

Article 23

Subject to and in accordance with the provisions of international conventions existing or hereafter to be agreed upon, the Members of the League:

(a) will endeavour to secure and maintain fair and humane conditions of labour for men, women, and children, both in their own countries and in all countries to which their commercial and industrial relations extend, and for that purpose will establish and maintain the necessary international organisations;

(b) undertake to secure just treatment of the native inhabitants of territories under their control;

(c) will entrust the League with the general supervision over the execution of agreements with regard to the traffic in women and children, and the traffic in opium and other dangerous drugs;

(d) will entrust the League with the general supervision of the trade in arms and ammunition with the countries in which the control of this traffic is necessary in the common interest;

(e) will make provision to secure and maintain freedom of communications and of transit and equitable treatment for the commerce of all Members of the League. In this connection, the special necessities of the regions devastated during the war of 1914–1918 shall be borne in mind;

(f) will endeavour to take steps in matters of international concern for the prevention and control of disease.

ARTICLE 24

THERE shall be placed under the direction of the League all international bureaux already established by general treaties if the parties to such treaties consent. All such international bureaux and all commissions for the regulation of matters of international interest hereafter constituted shall be placed under the direction of the League.

In all matters of international interest which are regulated by general conventions but which are not placed under the control of international bureaux or commissions, the Secretariat of the League shall, subject to the consent of the Council and if desired by the parties, collect and distribute all relevant information and shall render any other assistance which may be necessary or desirable.

The Council may include as part of the expenses of the Secretariat the expenses of any bureau or commission which is placed under the direction of the League.

ARTICLE 25

THE Members of the League agree to encourage and promote the establishment and co-operation of duly authorised voluntary national Red Cross organisations having as purposes the improvement of health, the prevention of disease and the mitigation of suffering throughout the world.

ARTICLE 26

AMENDMENTS to this Covenant will take effect when ratified by the Members of the League whose Representatives compose the Council and by a majority of the Members of the League whose Representatives compose the Assembly.

No such amendment shall bind any Member of the League which signifies its dissent therefrom, but in that case it shall cease to be a Member of the League.

APPENDIX IV

THE FOURTEEN POINTS[1]

THE program of the world's peace, therefore, is our program; and that program, the only possible program, as we see it, is this:

I. Open covenants of peace, openly arrived at, after which there shall be no private international understandings of any kind but diplomacy shall proceed always frankly and in the public view.

II. Absolute freedom of navigation upon the seas, outside territorial waters, alike in peace and in war, except as the seas may be closed in whole or in part by international action for the enforcement of international covenants.

III. The removal, so far as possible, of all economic barriers and the establishment of an equality of trade conditions among all the nations consenting to the peace and associating themselves for its maintenance.

IV. Adequate guarantees given and taken that national armaments will be reduced to the lowest point consistent with domestic safety.

V. A free, open-minded, and absolutely impartial adjustment of all colonial claims, based upon a strict observance of the principle that in determining all such questions of sovereignty the interests of the populations concerned must have equal weight with the equitable claims of the government whose title is to be determined.

VI. The evacuation of all Russian territory and such a settlement of all questions affecting Russia as will secure

[1] From the address of President Wilson delivered at a Joint Session of Congress on January 8, 1918.

the best and freest coöperation of the other nations of the world in obtaining for her an unhampered and unembarrassed opportunity for the independent determination of her own political development and national policy and assure her of a sincere welcome into the society of free nations under institutions of her own choosing; and, more than a welcome, assistance also of every kind that she may need and may herself desire. The treatment accorded Russia by her sister nations in the months to come will be the acid test of their good-will, of their comprehension of her needs as distinguished from their own interests, and of their intelligent and unselfish sympathy.

VII. Belgium, the whole world will agree, must be evacuated and restored, without any attempt to limit the sovereignty which she enjoys in common with all other free nations. No other single act will serve as this will serve to restore confidence among the nations in the laws which they have themselves set and determined for the government of their relations with one another. Without this healing act the whole structure and validity of international law is forever impaired.

VIII. All French territory should be freed and the invaded portions restored, and the wrong done to France by Prussia in 1871 in the matter of Alsace-Lorraine, which has unsettled the peace of the world for nearly fifty years, should be righted, in order that peace may once more be made secure in the interest of all.

IX. A readjustment of the frontiers of Italy should be effected along clearly recognizable lines of nationality.

X. The peoples of Austria-Hungary, whose place among the nations we wish to see safeguarded and assured, should be accorded the freest opportunity of autonomous development.

XI. Rumania, Serbia, and Montenegro should be evacuated; occupied territories restored; Serbia accorded free and secure access to the sea; and the relations of the several Balkan states to one another determined by friendly counsel along historically established lines of allegiance and nationality; and international guarantees of the political and economic independence and territorial integrity of the several Balkan states should be entered into.

XII. The Turkish portions of the present Ottoman Empire should be assured a secure sovereignty, but the other nationalities which are now under Turkish rule should be assured an undoubted security of life and an absolutely unmolested opportunity of autonomous development, and the Dardanelles should be permanently opened as a free passage to the ships and commerce of all nations under international guarantees.

XIII. An independent Polish state should be erected which should include the territories inhabited by indisputably Polish populations, which should be assured a free and secure access to the sea, and whose political and economic independence and territorial integrity should be guaranteed by international covenant.

XIV. A general association of nations must be formed under specific covenants for the purpose of affording mutual guarantees of political independence and territorial integrity to great and small states alike.

APPENDIX V

PRINCIPLES DECLARED BY PRESIDENT WILSON IN HIS ADDRESS OF FEBRUARY 11, 1918

THE principles to be applied are these:

First, that each part of the final settlement must be based upon the essential justice of that particular case and upon such adjustments as are most likely to bring a peace that will be permanent;

Second, that peoples and provinces are not to be bartered about from sovereignty to sovereignty as if they were mere chattels and pawns in a game, even the great game, now forever discredited, of the balance of power; but that

Third, every territorial settlement involved in this war must be made in the interest and for the benefit of the populations concerned, and not as a part of any mere adjustment or compromise of claims amongst rival states; and

Fourth, that all well defined national aspirations shall be accorded the utmost satisfaction that can be accorded them without introducing new or perpetuating old elements of discord and antagonism that would be likely in time to break the peace of Europe and consequently of the world.

APPENDIX VI

THE ARTICLES OF THE TREATY OF VERSAILLES RELATING TO SHANTUNG

ARTICLE 156

GERMANY renounces, in favour of Japan, all her rights, title and privileges — particularly those concerning the territory of Kiaochow, railways, mines, and submarine cables — which she acquired in virtue of the Treaty concluded by her with China on March 6, 1898, and of all other arrangements relative to the Province of Shantung.

All German rights in the Tsingtao-Tsinanfu Railway, including its branch lines, together with its subsidiary property of all kinds, stations, shops, fixed and rolling stock, mines, plant and material for the exploitation of the mines, are and remain acquired by Japan, together with all rights and privileges attaching thereto.

The German State submarine cables from Tsingtao to Shanghai and from Tsingtao to Chefoo, with all the rights, privileges and properties attaching thereto, are similarly acquired by Japan, free and clear of all charges and encumbrances.

ARTICLE 157

THE movable and immovable property owned by the German State in the territory of Kiaochow, as well as all the rights which Germany might claim in consequence of the works or improvements made or of the expenses incurred by her, directly or indirectly, in connection with this territory, are and remain acquired by Japan, free and clear of all charges and encumbrances.

ARTICLE 158

GERMANY shall hand over to Japan within three months from the coming into force of the present Treaty the archives, registers, plans, title-deeds and documents of every kind, wherever they may be, relating to the administration, whether civil, military, financial, judicial or other, of the territory of Kiaochow.

Within the same period Germany shall give particulars to Japan of all treaties, arrangements or agreements relating to the rights, title or privileges referred to in the two preceding Articles.

INDEX